311
311
MISSABE
311

Duluth, Missabe & Iron Range Railway

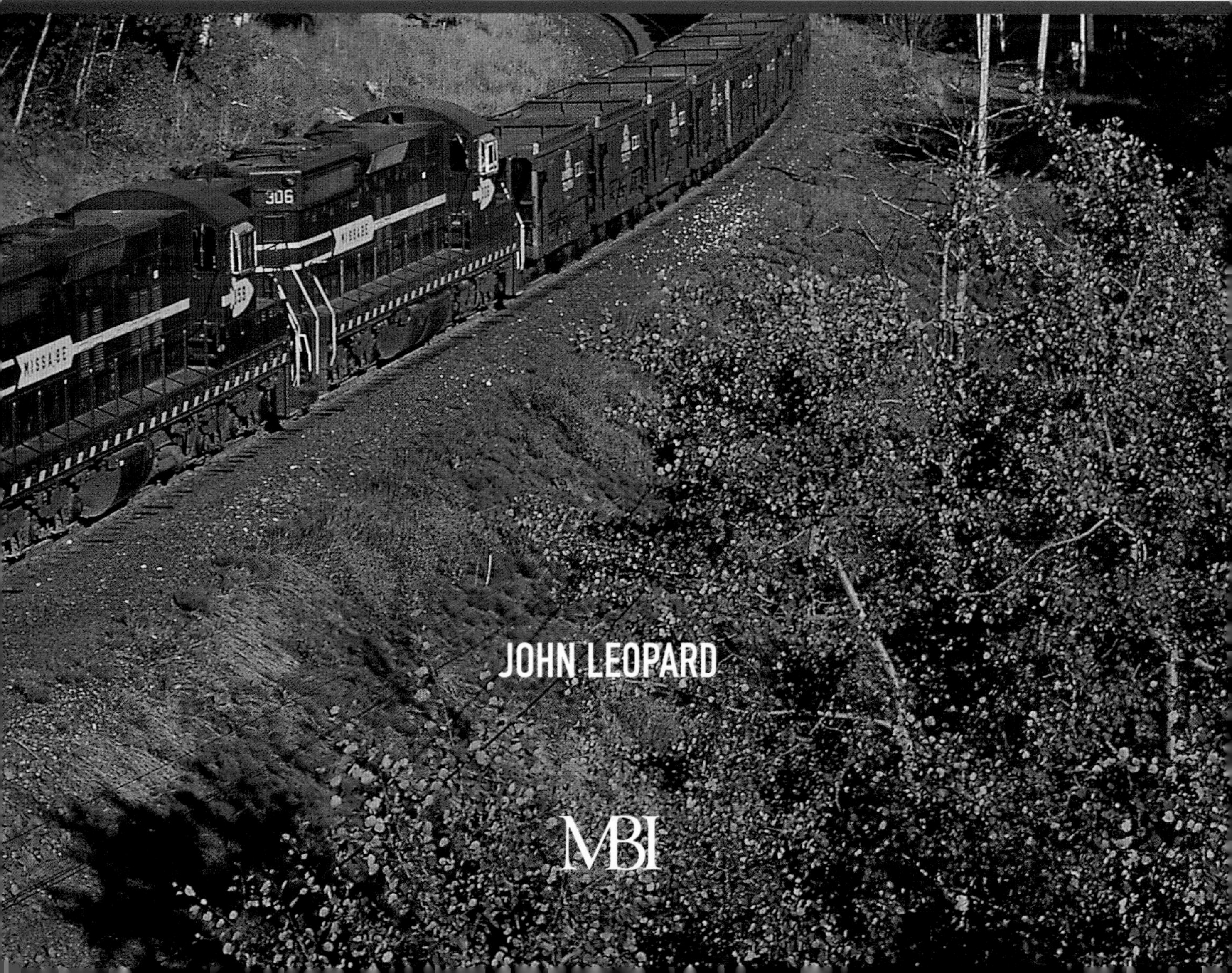

JOHN LEOPARD

MBI

Dedication

To my loving wife, Margo, and our wonderful children, Nathan and Lauryn.

First published in 2005 by MBI, an imprint of MBI Publishing Company, Galtier Plaza, Suite 200, 380 Jackson Street, St. Paul, MN 55101-3885 USA

© John Leopard, 2005

All rights reserved. With the exception of quoting brief passages for the purposes of review, no part of this publication may be reproduced without prior written permission from the Publisher.

The information in this book is true and complete to the best of our knowledge. All recommendations are made without any guarantee on the part of the author or Publisher, who also disclaim any liability incurred in connection with the use of this data or specific details.

This publication has not been prepared, approved, or licensed by Canadian National Railway Company. We recognize, further, that some words, model names, and designations mentioned herein are the property of the trademark holder. We use them for identification purposes only. This is not an official publication.

MBI titles are also available at discounts in bulk quantity for industrial or sales-promotional use. For details write to Special Sales Manager at MBI Publishing Company, Galtier Plaza, Suite 200, 380 Jackson Street, St. Paul, MN 55101-3885 USA.

ISBN-13: 978-0-7603-1762-4
ISBN-10: 0-7603-1762-3

Front cover: On October 3, 1991, a pair of SD38-2s (Nos. 209 and 213) pulls a trainload of Minorca pellets through Sax en route to the docks at Duluth. The Missabe acquired both locomotives in April 1975. *John Leopard*

Frontis: Loads and empties meet on the two-main track CTC between Jones and Gilbert in August 1991, as seen from Highway 135 east of Gilbert. SD38-2 No. 213 heads up the three-unit set powering a loaded train from Minntac to Two Harbors. *John Leopard*

Title pages: On the afternoon of August 20, 1995, Missabe's 15:30 Hill Ore job approaches the Boundary Avenue overpass at the top of Proctor Hill. In the distance are the St. Louis River and the city of Superior, Wisconsin. *John Leopard*

Back cover: Santa Fe–type No. 504 switches a cut of cabooses at Proctor on May 17, 1956. One of the Missabe's Santa Fes, No. 506, was donated to the National Railroad Museum in Green Bay, Wisconsin, in 1962. *Robert C. Anderson* ***Inset:*** A DM&IR worker thaws ore cars at Proctor in 1956. *Basgen Photography, David C. Schauer collection*

Editor: Dennis Pernu
Designer: Chris Fayers

Printed in Hong Kong

Contents

ACKNOWLEDGMENTS

The few words written here cannot begin to convey my appreciation to the following individuals who made this book better in every way. My right-hand man has been David Schauer. An accomplished photographer, this lifelong fan of the Missabe Road has done much to preserve the company's history with his efforts at the Missabe Railroad Historical Society, both as the group's president and as editor of its magazine *Ore Extra*.

Two DM&IR employees, Mike Urie and Thomas C. Sample, were instrumental in helping with the operational and locomotive aspects of the book's text. I was fortunate to work in the DM&IR dispatcher's office at Keenan for a brief period in my career and made a few friends while I was there. I wish them all good luck in their post-DM&IR lives.

Several photographers were kind enough to dig through their collections and find the images included here. Their names are scattered with their photos throughout this volume, and I am forever grateful for their efforts in sharing them. Providing assistance in locating historical photos were Scott Kuzma and Aimee Brown at the Iron Range Research Center at Ironworld in Chisholm, Minnesota, and Kathy Bergan at the Iron Range Historical Society in Gilbert, Minnesota. Thanks, also, to Dan Mackey, who hooked me up with Mike Schmid and the Basgen Photo Archives.

Providing valuable input concerning the mining aspects of the text was Bruce Kettunen.

Thanks to this book's editor, Dennis Pernu, for his guidance thoughout, and to Brian Solomon for recommending me to Dennis for this project.

Three Missabe SD38s wheel a train of taconite pellets through a curve at the west end of Biwabik in August 1991. This train, loaded at U.S. Steel's Minntac pellet plant, is destined for unloading at the docks at Two Harbors. *John Leopard*

INTRODUCTION

On the warm, tranquil afternoon of July 19, 1991, the 15:30 Hill Ore job pulls off Dock No. 6 with empty ore cars and rounds the curve at Collingwood (in Duluth). Upon arriving at Proctor Yard, this crew will exchange the empty cars for another set of loads to bring down Proctor Hill. On most afternoons the Hill Ore made three roundtrips between Proctor Yard and the Duluth docks. Taconite stockpiles of the Lakehead Taconite Storage Facility can be seen over the top of the train, with St. Louis Bay and Lake Superior in the distance. *John Leopard*

Minnesota's Iron Range country and the Duluth, Missabe & Iron Range Railway have always held a strong fascination for students of railroading. The specialized requirements of hauling iron ore and taconite pellets—which are found and manufactured, respectively, in few other places—contribute to this interest. But the story of the DM&IR, or, as it is more popularly known, the Missabe Road, is much more than locomotives, ore cars, and rail lines—it is also a story of Great Lakes shipping, ore docks, mines, steel production, and of the nation's economy.

Iron Ore = Steel: A Reason for Being

Iron is one of the world's most plentiful elements; it makes up nearly 5 percent of the earth's crust. Yet few places have it in quantities concentrated enough for it to be mined economically. Iron, the element, is needed to produce what is called metallic iron. The process of making metallic iron, also known as pig iron, from iron ore is called smelting, which is done in a blast furnace. The blast furnace is where the iron is freed from the ore. In simple terms, the blast furnace is where raw materials—such as iron ore, limestone, and coke—are melted down by continuously

A view of a small portion of the blast furnace and associated heat-generating tanks at U.S. Steel's Duluth Works mill, once an important DM&IR customer. *Basgen Photography, Tom Dorin collection*

blasting air heated to temperatures of 3,000 degrees Fahrenheit. At the bottom of the blast furnace, a pool of white-hot molten pig iron collects as the lighter impurities in the ore float to the top. Steel is made by further refining the pig iron by removing certain elements and remaining impurities, such as carbon, silicon, and phosphorus.

Northern Minnesota is one of the few places where nature buried iron deposits rich enough for mining. To date, iron ore shipments from Minnesota have been over 4 billion tons, ranking it among the largest sources of iron ore in the world. While shipments of about 200 million tons a year each from Brazil and Australia have dwarfed Minnesota as the largest iron ore producer in the last 20 years, Minnesota still ships a respectable 40 to 45 million tons a year of iron ore pellets. Of this, the Missabe handles about 23 million tons a year.

Like most metals, iron is almost always found in combination with other elements and is further complicated with amounts of earth matter, chiefly sand and clay. Unlike most metals, which are usually chemically combined with sulfur, iron is chemically combined with oxygen.

Minnesota's iron ranges were conceived over two billion years ago when a huge, shallow sea covered the area that is today northeastern Minnesota. Over time, thick layers of iron-bearing sediments settled to the bottom of this sea. As the waters disappeared these sediments were buried under thousands of feet of sand, clay, and mud. This deep burial subjected the iron-rich sediments to heat and pressure, compressing them into a hard silica-based rock called taconite. In what is now the eastern Mesabi Range, heat from later lava flows converted the original iron mineral in the rock to magnetite, the iron-bearing mineral. Magnetic taconite consists primarily of quartzite (a form of silica) and magnetite, a black or grayish magnetic iron mineral.

During the long period of its formation, the taconite rock was subjected to a variety of geologic events. When this area of the earth's crust rose, the overburden was largely scraped off by glacial action, exposing portions of the iron-rich formations to the atmosphere. As rainfall and glacial-melt waters percolated through some areas of the exposed taconite, some of the silica in the taconite dissolved and was carried away. This converted the hard gray taconite into pockets of soft red-colored hematite, also known as "natural ore." The iron content of high-grade natural ore could be 55 to 65 percent; the iron content of taconite rock varies, but is seldom more than 35 percent.

Iron ore is the main ingredient in the production of steel. As the United States industrialized during the second half of the nineteenth century, the demand for steel grew and so did the need for iron ore. Mines in New England supplied the raw material for weapons of the Revolutionary War, and as the American population spread westward, new iron mines discovered in Kentucky and Ohio met the needs of an expanding frontier. While steel was expensive to make, the need for iron in a growing country spurred technological improvements in steel-making and stimulated the search for new sources of iron ore.

In 1856 an efficient means of making steel from iron was introduced almost simultaneously by Henry Bessemer, an English ironmaster, and William Kelley, from Kentucky. Each discovered that steel could be made cheaply from iron by blowing superheated air at high velocity through the molten iron, thus burning off the impurities, mainly silicon and carbon. This process, named for Bessemer, was the first economical method for making large quantities of steel. Removing impurities gave steel greater strength and hardness than wrought iron, which up to that point was the most prevalent metal made for industrial use. The Bessemer process was quickly followed by a method known as open-hearth, which in turn was followed by the basic oxygen process that continues to form the basis for modern steel production.

New Sources of Ore

During the last half of the nineteenth century, large high-grade iron ore deposits were found in upper Michigan and northern Wisconsin in what became the Marquette, Menominee, and Gogebic iron ranges. The first shipment from the Marquette Range occurred in 1852; Menominee developed in the mid-1870s and the Gogebic a decade later. These reserves became available to the steel-making centers of Pennsylvania and Ohio after the federal government made money available to the state of Michigan to construct a canal and locks at Sault Ste. Marie. This canal allowed boats to bypass the rapids of the St. Mary's River and negotiate the 22-foot difference in water levels between Lake Superior and Lakes Huron and Michigan. After the locks were opened on June 18, 1855, Great Lakes shipping flourished, with the Soo Locks soon becoming the busiest such installation in the world.

As the young nation's industrial capacity grew, the mining companies looked westward for more raw materials. The first of Minnesota's natural ore deposits to be commercially developed was the Vermilion Range, nearly 25 miles long and 2 miles wide, and located 75 miles northeast of Duluth. At nearly 2.7 billion years of age, it was Minnesota's oldest iron ore formation. The Vermilion Range was set apart from other Minnesota ranges by its hard lump ores that were among the richest in terms of iron content, ranging upwards of 65 percent. At first the mines were open-pit style, but by the early 1890s all had shifted underground as the mines deepened.

An early-1894 view of the Iron King Mine near Virginia shows the original open pit. All stripping and mining operations were done by hand until the introduction of steam-powered shovels on the Mesabi Range in 1892. *Iron Range Historical Society, Gilbert, Minnesota*

A circa-1966 view of molten metal from a blast furnace pouring from a ladle to charge an open-hearth furnace at the U.S. Steel Duluth Works. *Basgen Photography, Tom Dorin collection*

Oliver Iron Mining Company steam locomotive No. 543, with an 0-8-0 wheel arrangement, spots cars for loading at the Morrison Mine near Coleraine in September 1947. The dipper of this electric-powered shovel had a 5-cubic-yard capacity. The first steam-powered shovel brought to the Mesabi Range was used at the Biwabik Mine in 1892. *Iron Range Research Center, Chisholm, Minnesota*

Hauling taconite pellets, unlike raw ore, is a year-round affair. On January 30, 1991, an empty train makes its own snowstorm while approaching Gilbert on the Iron Range Division mainline. *John Leopard*

The next area of iron ore to be developed in Minnesota was the Mesabi Range. The word *Mesabi*—variously spelled Mesaba, Missabay, and Missabe (the form adopted by the railroad)—is derived from the Ojibwe Indian word for "sleeping giant." The Mesabi grew to become the largest of Minnesota's iron ranges and has provided over 95 percent of all iron ore shipped from Minnesota. At just over 100 miles in length, the Mesabi Range consists of a thick layer of taconite varying in width from 1 to 3 miles and reaching a depth of up to 600 feet. While many of the mines on the Mesabi Range started out as underground operations, its softer natural ore was at a shallower depth than the harder ores of the Vermilion Range; thus, with the development of the steam shovel, the majority of mines on the Mesabi are open pit.

The third of Minnesota's iron ranges to be developed was the Cuyuna Range, which shipped its first ore in 1911. Located about 100 miles west of Duluth, the Cuyuna was served by the Northern Pacific railroad, and later the Burlington Northern and Soo Line railroads. However, the DM&IR did have a hand in Cuyuna ore—when BN converted its ore docks at Allouez, Wisconsin, just east of Superior, to handle nothing but taconite in 1979, the natural ore shipments that remained from either the BN or the Soo Line were interchanged to the DM&IR and dumped on its ore docks at Duluth. This arrangement lasted until the last Cuyuna ore was shipped in the fall of 1984.

A fourth Minnesota iron range was also developed, this one in southern Minnesota: the Fillmore County District, which shipped over 8 million tons of ore from 1941 to 1969. This district was located near Spring Valley, Minnesota, near the Iowa border. Fillmore County ore was shipped on the Chicago Great Western Railroad to mills near Chicago and St. Louis.

CHAPTER ONE

BIRTH OF AN ORE HAULER

One of DM&IR's massive Yellowstone-type steam locomotives, DM&IR Class M-4 No. 230, runs southward with a long string of loaded cars on the Missabe Division at Burnett on May 16, 1959. These articulated behemoths were said to be patterned after a Western Pacific 2-8-8-2 design, but the Missabe's desire for a roomier cab brought about an increase in weight, necessitating a four-wheel trailing truck. *Robert C. Anderson*

Duluth & Iron Range Railroad

Natural iron ore was first observed in the vicinity of Lake Vermilion, Minnesota, as early as 1850. Nothing much was made of this until 15 years later, when reports of gold brought prospectors rushing to the area. Around 1865 a community named Winston City was established near the southeast shore of Lake Vermilion, and during this time as many as 16 mining enterprises sought their fortunes in gold. Little gold was actually found, however, and the boom was over by 1867.

Nevertheless, some of the prospectors did take note of the iron formations that had been found but ignored in the quest for instant wealth. High-grade iron deposits were reported at several locations around Lake Vermilion and southward, near the site of the present-day town of Babbitt. Lumbering companies were soon active in the area as well; the forests of northern Michigan were rapidly being depleted, while the stands of white pine that stood atop the Vermilion and Mesabi iron deposits remained uncut.

After a few failed initial attempts at developing the Lake Vermilion deposits, the high iron content of the Vermilion Range ores caught the interest of Philadelphia lawyer and capitalist Charlemagne Tower. Tower began assembling most of the prime properties of the Vermilion Range, forming his Minnesota Iron Company on December 1, 1882. Tower realized a railroad connecting the Vermilion Range with Lake Superior was necessary if the ore was to have any value.

Tower formed the Duluth and Iron Mountain Railroad in 1881, but could not

A circa-1918 view of ore mining at the Sellers Mine, one of the massive group of mines collectively known as the Hull-Rust Mine near Hibbing. Many of the mining companies maintained their own fleet of cars and locomotives. Nearly 100 miles of track spiraled down into the depths of the Hull-Rust Mine. *Iron Range Historical Society, Gilbert, Minnesota*

Electric-powered shovels were introduced to the Mesabi Range mines in 1924. Upward of 10 men were needed to operate a steam-powered shovel, where only three men were needed to dig with an early-era electric shovel. Here, Oliver Iron Mining Company steamer No. 518 positions a cut of steel cars for a Marion-built electric-powered shovel at an unspecified Mesabi Range open-pit mining operation. *Iron Range Research Center, Chisholm, Minnesota*

convince the state legislature to grant him a charter. So Tower went about it another way, gaining control of a previously authorized charter that had failed to produce as intended. This charter carried the name Duluth & Iron Range Railroad Company, which another group had formed in 1874 to build a line northwest from Duluth toward the international boundary and a connection with the

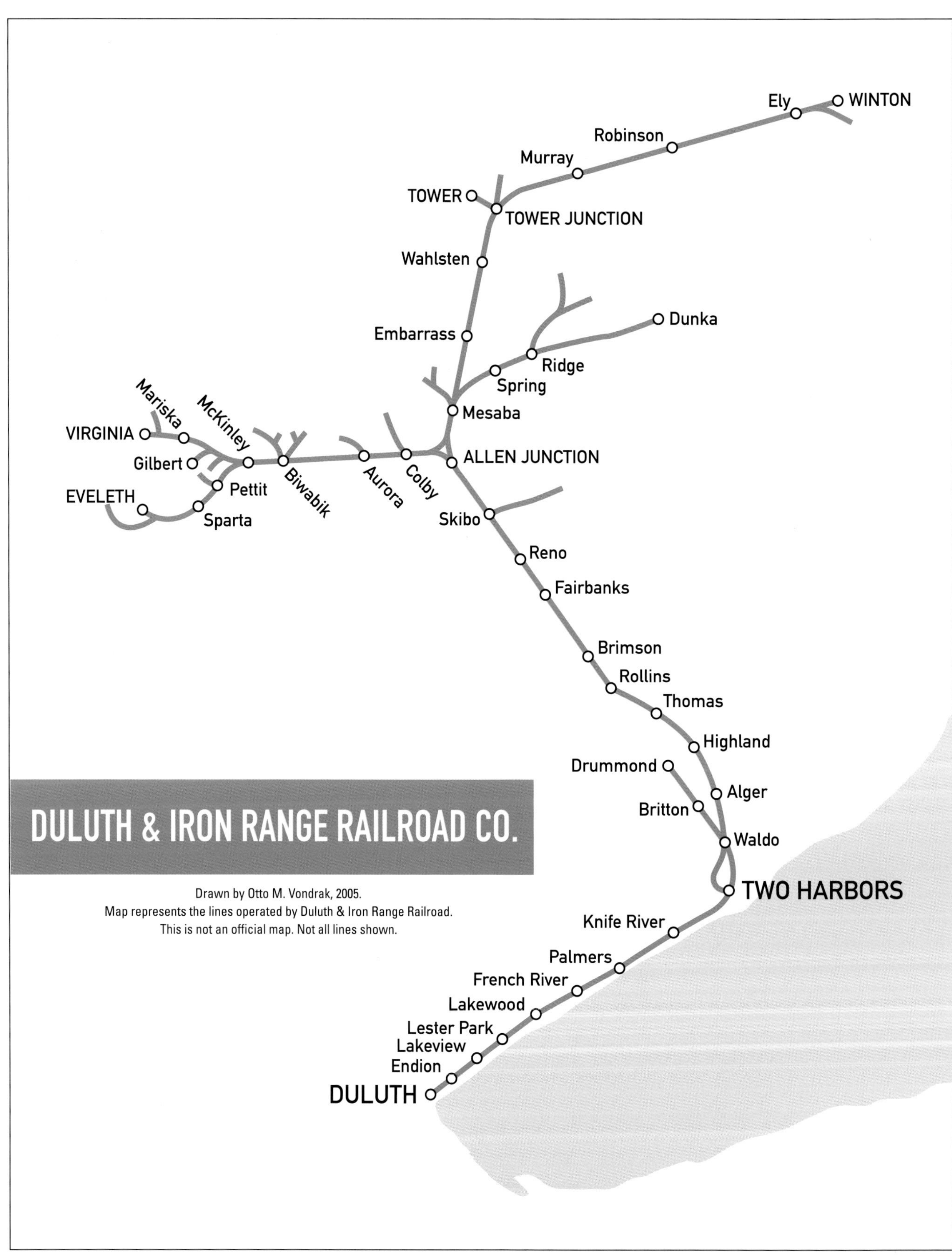
WINTON
Ely
Robinson
Murray
TOWER
TOWER JUNCTION
Wahlsten
Dunka
Embarrass
Ridge
Spring
Mesaba
Mariska
McKinley
VIRGINIA
Gilbert
Pettit
EVELETH
Sparta
Biwabik
Aurora
Colby
ALLEN JUNCTION
Skibo
Reno
Fairbanks
Brimson
Rollins
Thomas
Highland
Drummond
Alger
Britton
Waldo
TWO HARBORS
Knife River
Palmers
French River
Lakewood
Lester Park
Lakeview
Endion
DULUTH
DULUTH & IRON RANGE RAILROAD CO.
Drawn by Otto M. Vondrak, 2005.
Map represents the lines operated by Duluth & Iron Range Railroad.
This is not an official map. Not all lines shown.

Three ships being loaded at Two Harbors on a busy morning in spring 1981. The closest is U.S. Steel's first large ore-hauling vessel, the *Roger Blough*, launched in 1972 and stretching 858 feet in length. The *Blough* was a precursor to U.S. Steel's two 1,000-foot-long vessels that followed in 1979 and 1980. Tied up at the short dock closest to the shoreline is DM&IR's steam-powered tugboat, *Edna G*, which was retired in 1981 and donated to the city of Two Harbors. *Basgen Photography, Dan Mackey collection*

Canadian Pacific, which was then being built. Tower sought legislative approval to change the original charter's terminal from Duluth to Agate Bay (later renamed Two Harbors). Approval to make the required route changes was granted by the Minnesota House of Representatives on March 1, 1883, and surveys were soon begun for a direct route linking Agate Bay with Tower's iron ore holdings to the north. On June 20, 1883, John S. Wolf was awarded a contract to construct a 68-mile line between the two points.

Tower had meanwhile begun mining operations to ensure that ore could be loaded the day the railroad was ready to accept shipments. The first mining activity was conducted at a place called the Soudan Mine, near the town of Tower. One hundred and forty men were working the mine in April 1884, this increased to some 540 men by June of that same year. The first rail shipment from the Soudan Mine was made on July 31, 1884, and consisted of 10 cars, each carrying 20 tons of iron ore. At first the mining operation was open pit, but underground mining began in 1888 at Soudan and soon after all mining operations on the Vermilion Range followed

Steam generator–equipped SD9s 129 and 130 lead a Lake Superior Museum of Transportation–sponsored excursion train past the Endion Depot on July 26, 1975. The depot was constructed for the D&IR in 1899 and saw its last regular scheduled passenger train on July 15, 1961. Due to its unique and handsome architecture, the building was placed on the National Register of Historic Places in April 1975. After the depot was retired from railroad service it was sold to a private firm in 1980 and later moved in 1987 to a nearby site. Until recently, it served as offices for the Duluth Convention and Visitors Bureau. *Steve Glischinski*

the ore underground as the rich veins became too deep to reach via open pits.

The first ore dock at Agate Bay, built of timber in 1884, had a capacity of 16,000 tons in 162 pockets. A second ore dock, also built of timber and completed a year later, was of slightly greater capacity, with 18,000 tons of storage capacity in 141 large pockets. Several merchandise docks and a coal dock were completed by 1890. To support the railroad, the Minnesota Iron Company constructed a roundhouse and repair facility in what had by then become Two Harbors. Because there was no road or rail connection from Duluth to Agate Bay, all supplies and railroad equipment were carried by boat and barge along the north shore of Lake Superior.

Steel companies had begun to accept the Vermilion ore, which had a very high iron content, averaging 68 percent by weight, and a low phosphorous content, which was also very desirable. At the close of 1885, construction of a third dock was under way at Two Harbors as ore shipments continued to climb, with 227,075 tons shipped that year. In addition, a contract was let to build a 26-mile extension, the Lake Division, along the north shore of Lake Superior to connect Two Harbors with Duluth. This line was completed during December 1886. The Lake Division served as a vital link to bring in supplies and crews for mining and rail expansion on the Vermilion Range.

The success of the Minnesota Iron Company didn't go unnoticed. A syndicate directed by H. H. Porter (of the Illinois Steel Company and also a director of the Pullman Palace Car Company), Marshall Field (of the Chicago mercantile empire that bore his name), Cyrus McCormick (the well-known farm-implement manufacturer), and John D. Rockefeller (the owner of Standard Oil) took interest. Their own search for a source of high-grade iron ore led to the acquisition of deposits about 20 miles east of Tower, near Ely.

In an attempt to squeeze Tower out of the Vermilion Range, the Porter syndicate gave Charlemagne Tower an ultimatum: either sell them the D&IR or they would build a competing line. In April 1887, Tower reluctantly sold his mining and railroad complex to the Illinois Steel Company for $6.4 million, doubling his investment in just five years. At the time, the D&IR had 95 miles of track in operation using 13 locomotives and 340 ore cars.

With an almost inexhaustible source of capital to tap, massive improvements to the D&IR came quickly. A car shop at Two Harbors was built that soon began turning out a large fleet of 24-foot wooden ore cars. A 21-mile extension from the town of Tower to the Porter syndicate's Chandler Mine near Ely was completed in the summer of 1888. This line was extended 4 miles to mines near Winton in 1894. Prior to the end of the nineteenth century, four more mines, the Pioneer, Zenith, Savoy, and Sibley, were operating in the area, each contributing to the D&IR's tonnage.

During the 1890s two more timber ore docks were built at Two Harbors, bringing the number of ore docks there to five. Dock No. 5 contained 168 pockets and was 54 feet high, making it the largest, and the last, timber ore dock built at Two Harbors. In 1892 more than a million tons of ore were shipped from Two Harbors, its best year to that date.

On June 24, 1979, eastbound taconite loads come into Biwabik behind SD18 No. 189. This train is operating eastbound on the X Branch, which was part of D&IR's Western Mesaba Branch between Allen Junction/Wyman and McKinley, with tracks continuing on from there to either Virginia on the X Branch or Eveleth via the Z Branch. Curving to the left is track of the former DM&N Biwabik Branch that started at Iron Junction. The remaining rails of the X Branch between Biwabik and McKinley and the Z Branch from McKinley to Jones were removed in 1991. *Robert C. Anderson*

204
204

Just outside Two Harbors, the "Loop Line," or Northward track, passes over the former D&IR line to Duluth, later to be operated by the North Shore Scenic Railroad. The Loop Line, separated from the Southward track by up to a mile and a half, was built to bypass the nearly 3 percent grades that the original mainline encountered while leaving the Lake Superior Basin. On June 9, 1992, an empty train tackles the 1.5 percent grade on the Northward track while leaving Two Harbors. ***John Leopard***

The discovery of soft, mineable ore on the Mesabi Range required westward expansion of the D&IR. At first the company surveyed a new line that would run from a point 2 miles west of Two Harbors to Eveleth. But this plan was deemed too expensive and was never built. A cheaper alternative was the railroad's initial foray into the Mesabi Range called the Western Mesaba Branch, an 18-mile line from the mainline at Wyman to McKinley (near Biwabik) built in 1892. It was extended the next year to Virginia, and in 1894 a line connecting McKinley with Eveleth was completed. Additional extensions were built in this area in the 1890s to serve new mines on the Mesabi Range's east end.

Opposite: **Near the Waldo station, 4 miles north of Two Harbors, the Northward and Southward mains, as they were labeled in the employee timetable, join. On June 9, 1992, an empty train destined for Minntac operates on the Northward track at Waldo. The steep grade, just shy of 3 percent, down the original D&IR mainline (Southward track) to Two Harbors and lake level is seen to the left.** ***John Leopard***

To ease the movement of ore trains, the entire mainline between Two Harbors and Allen Junction was double-tracked during 1899. In addition, the mainline was relocated between Rollins and Waldo, and the "Loop Line" was built at Two Harbors. These projects reduced the 3 percent northbound ruling grade out of Two Harbors to 1.5 percent and helped ease the D&IR's undulating profile. Orders were placed for the company's first all-steel ore cars in 1899, each with a capacity of 50 tons. When 1900 rolled around, D&IR tonnage figures had reached nearly 4 million, split almost evenly between mines on the Vermilion and Mesabi ranges. Ironically, given the consolidations to come, the D&IR's expansions into the eastern Mesabi were often in direct competition with the Duluth, Missabe & Northern Railroad.

Duluth, Missabe & Northern Railroad

Preliminary exploration for iron ore on the Mesabi Range was largely confined to the range's east end. Here, the preponderance of deposits were composed of hard, low-grade taconite, commercially useless at the time. Many believed that the high-grade ore of the Vermilion Range wasn't to be found on the Mesabi, so prospecting there was sporadic. As early as 1866, Henry H. Eames, Minnesota's first state geologist, made the first widely known references to finding red iron ore on the Mesabi Range. However, subsequent reports of iron ore findings on the Mesabi Range continued to relate its unfavorable commercial value.

Lewis H. Merritt of Duluth believed otherwise. After obtaining samples of iron ore on a trip through the Mesabi, he determined that high-grade hematite existed there in quantity. Persuaded by their father's notions, three of Merritt's sons extensively prospected the Mesabi Range beginning in 1885. Their efforts paid off five years later, when on November 16, 1890, they discovered the first large deposit of soft ore on the Mesabi Range at a location they named Mountain Iron. The following year two woodsmen discovered iron ore at the base of an uprooted tree near Biwabik, 20 miles east of Mountain Iron. The Merritts soon leased this land and developed what became known as the Biwabik Mine. They also found a large body of soft ore near Virginia, which was named the Missabe Mountain Mine. Any doubts that the Mesabi Range was blessed with deposits of soft natural ore were soon erased.

Not wanting to be burdened with building and operating a railroad, the Merritts approached the Northern Pacific and the St. Paul & Duluth railroads to build branchlines to their mines, but these roads were more interested in their own expansion affairs. After

An early view at Alborn shows heavy passenger traffic as three trains congregate in front of the wooden station. Just south of Alborn was Coleraine Junction and the jumping-off point for the Alborn Branch. This 55-mile line led northwest toward the mines on the western end of the Mesabi Range. *Iron Range Historical Society, Gilbert, Minnesota*

When most railroads were buying new diesel locomotives, the Missabe was still acquiring used steam engines from other U.S. Steel-owned railroads. Eighteen large Texas-type (2-10-4) steamers came from the Bessemer & Lake Erie in 1951. Numbered 700 through 717 on the DM&IR, they were considered the largest two-cylindered locomotives ever built. No. 715 rests at the Proctor coaling tower on a crisp November 14, 1959. ***Robert C. Anderson***

their failed attempts to entice an established railroad company, the Merritts chose to build their own line, and on February 11, 1891, the Duluth, Missabe & Northern Railway Company was incorporated to build a 48-mile line due south from Mountain Iron to a connection with the Duluth & Winnipeg Railroad at Stoney Brook Junction, near Brookston. Operating headquarters for the DM&N were located at Iron Junction, where an engine house and car repair facilities were constructed. At the time, the D&W was operating just over 100 miles of track from Superior, Wisconsin, west to Deer River, Minnesota. An agreement was made on April 14, 1892, for the D&W to handle DM&N traffic between Stoney Brook Junction and an ore dock to be constructed at Allouez, Wisconsin. The D&W would later become a key component of the Great Northern Railway, which was to become a very large iron ore transporter in its own right; today Allouez is Burlington Northern Santa Fe's iron ore shipping port.

Shortly after surveys were completed, the crews of contractor Donald Grant began preparing the DM&N's roadbed. Much of the line traversed a great, uninhabited swamp, requiring extensive fills. Sixty-pound rail was spiked down beginning in July, and the line was complete to Mountain Iron by October 1892. Grant next laid an 18-mile branch from Iron Junction to Biwabik, where the Merritts controlled most of the high-grade deposits with their Biwabik Mine, the first large-scale open-pit mine on the Mesabi. Also completed in 1892 was a 6-mile branch from Wolf, just north of Iron Junction, to the Missabe Mountain Mine. In the summer of that year, the Missabe Mountain Mine was leased to Pittsburgh industrialist Henry W. Oliver, who in turn leased other iron-mining properties all across the developing Mesabi Range and formed his own Oliver Iron Mining Company in September 1892.

The Merritts' first 10 carloads of Mesabi Range ore arrived in Allouez on October 18, 1892, via the Duluth & Winnipeg. One car was promptly sent from the yard at Allouez to Duluth where it was put on display under the train shed at Union Depot for all to see. When this first shipment of ore from the Mountain Iron Mine arrived at Allouez, the D&W's timber dock was still incomplete but would ultimately have 100 pockets, each holding 180 tons of ore. Upon the dock's completion, a cargo of 2,078 tons was loaded on November 11, 1892, into a waiting whaleback barge. Only one additional vessel was loaded prior to a shutdown of operations brought on by winter weather. That first season, 4,245 tons of Mountain Iron Mine ore was shipped, all consigned to Oglebay, Norton and Company of Cleveland, Ohio.

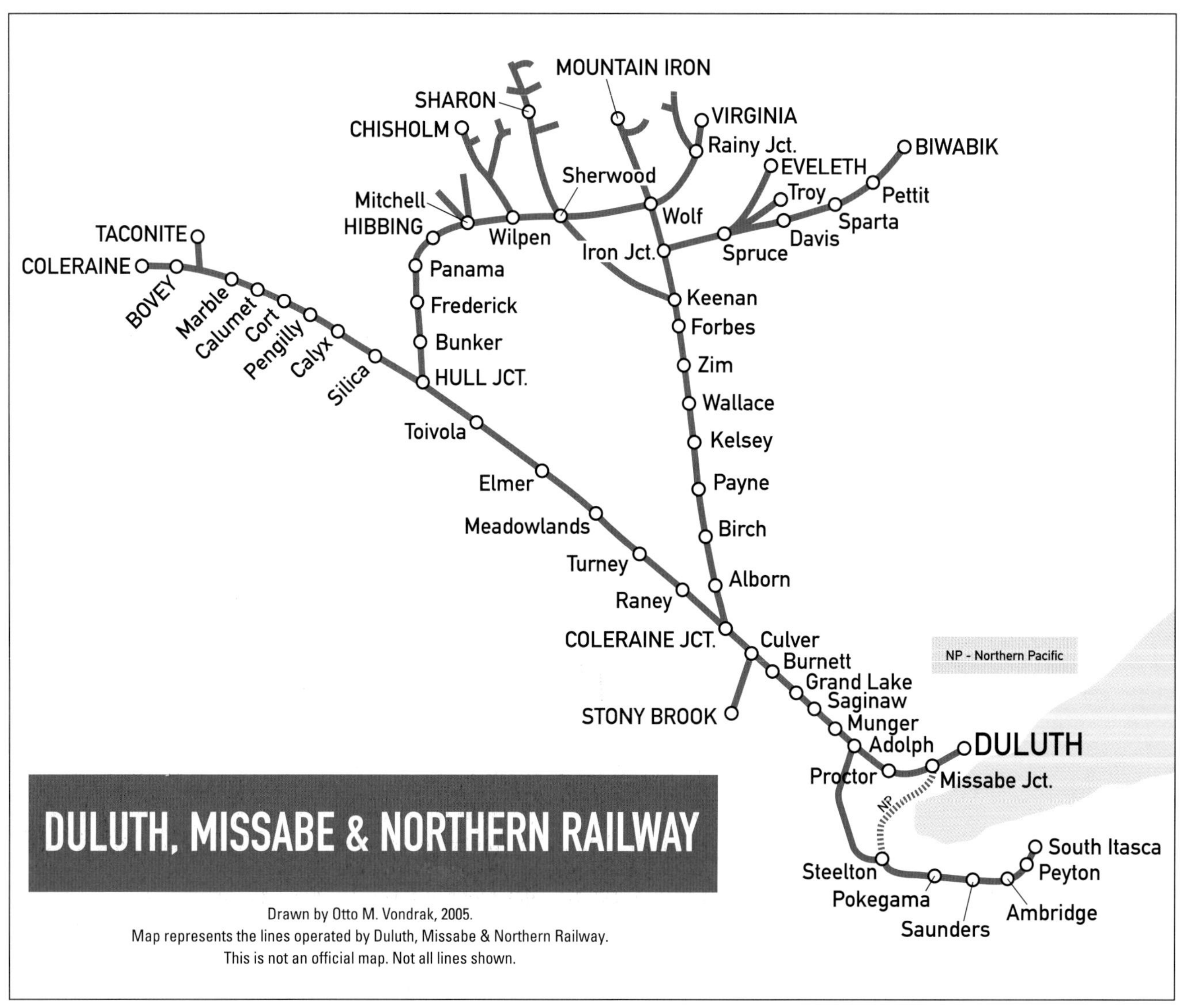

This view of Proctor Yard, looking southeast from the car shop area, was taken in 1959. An interesting collection of freight cars is present, and the concrete coaling tower built in 1916 looms in the distance. The tower was removed in the summer of 1970 to make way for a new yard office and operations center. *Basgen Photography, author collection*

The Merritts were devoted to their adopted home city of Duluth and had always intended their railroad to terminate there. They soon became dissatisfied with the handling D&W gave their ore, claiming that the D&W was not complying with its promise to supply DM&N with enough ore cars for its shipping needs. Not wanting to forfeit their ore delivery contracts, the Merritts began construction of the Duluth Extension. In March 1893, contractors began to clear the right-of-way between Columbia Junction (on the existing line northeast of Stoney Brook) and Duluth. The section of this extension between Proctor and Duluth would descend 600 feet down the lakeshore escarpment into Duluth. This 2.2 percent grade was named Proctor Hill and soon became a limiting factor in operations; to ease operating headaches, a second main track

Amply illustrating the rugged climb up Proctor Hill, the May 27, 1989, version of the Hill Ore claws up the 2.2 percent grade and crosses over Interstate 35. A nice mixture of motive power is present in the form of SD-M No. 304, SD18 No. 179, SD38AC No. 201, and SD9 No. 159. Duluth's landmark Aerial Lift Bridge is far in the distance, marking the entrance to the Duluth Harbor. *Mike Cleary*

was constructed on Proctor Hill just months after the first track was completed.

The rail connection to Duluth from Columbia Junction, a 36-track receiving yard at Proctor, and an enormous timber dock were completed by midsummer 1893, and on July 22 the first train of Mesabi ore shipped entirely over DM&N tracks—10 cars of rich hematite from the Mountain Iron Mine—arrived in Duluth. The ore was dumped into the dock, which was then the largest of its kind in the world. A half-mile-long

trestle connected the 2,304-foot-long dock to shore, with the dock's 384 pockets each holding 125 tons. Unfortunately for the Merritts, their timing was terrible—the country was sliding into a financial crisis known as the Panic of 1893.

As the economic climate worsened, the Merritts overextended their finances and began relying on John D. Rockefeller for operating capital. Rockefeller's involvement began with his help financing the extension to Duluth and by October 1893 included funds

Mitchell Yard, just east of Hibbing, was the major staging area supporting the eastern half of the great Hull-Rust group of mines. Mitchell had a three-stall engine house, as well as coaling and watering facilities to handle the concentration of locomotives assigned to this terminal. June 15, 1957, finds Santa Fe-type No. 509 pulling into the yard with a train of empty ore cars. *Bud Bulgrin*

necessary to construct the Superior Branch from Wolf westward to important mines near Hibbing. At this time the DM&N comprised 116 route miles, plus 7 miles of second track on Proctor Hill.

On July 21, 1893, the Lake Superior Consolidated Iron Mines Company was formed to straighten out the complex financial affair between the Merritts and Rockefeller. However, the Merritts were on the verge of financial ruin and soon sold out completely to Rockefeller. In February 1894, Rockefeller assumed control of both the DM&N and the Merritts' mining properties, and improvements and additions were undertaken at once. The mainline, much of it already sinking into the swamps, was extensively reworked, eliminating increasingly frequent derailments of the heavy ore trains. An expanded ore-sorting yard at Proctor was completed in 1895, and construction of a second timber ore dock at Duluth was begun late that year. Smaller than the first dock, which had a 55,000-ton capacity, the second dock had 192 pockets and held a total of 35,000 tons.

Additional branch trackage was constructed as new iron mines were opened in

rapid succession at Virginia, Eveleth, Biwabik, and farther west near Hibbing. Almost two million tons of ore were shipped through the two DM&N docks at Duluth in 1896. With tonnages increasing every year, improvements were constant; 1900 proved to be a watershed year with many new improvements in the works. Crews began a project that would bring about the double-tracking of the mainline between Proctor and Wolf: 6 miles of second track were laid between Wolf and Shaw with 4.6 miles of second main laid north from Proctor. In addition, Dock No. 3 in Duluth was built that year, 15 miles of 60-pound mainline rail were relaid with 80 pound rail, and 800 new 35-ton wooden ore cars were purchased. These were the last wooden cars acquired by the DM&N, as five experimental all-steel ore cars were introduced in 1900.

EMD delivered SD9s 159 through 174 early in the spring of 1959, rounding out DM&IR's purchase of that model. June 4, 1988, finds a pair of SD9s from that final order, Nos. 164 and 167, leading an SD-M and a train of loaded cars at the south end of Proctor Yard. Visible above the ore cars in the distance are buildings of the original steam-era back shops and roundhouse. ***Mike Cleary***

Missabe's Steelton Switch eases into Steelton on a fine September morning in 2003. This job operates on Wednesday and Sunday mornings out of Proctor Yard, making a roundtrip to the C&NW/UP interchange at South Itasca. *David C. Schauer*

CHAPTER TWO

INTO A NEW CENTURY

Iron mining and steel-making became big business as the twentieth century dawned. Small operators didn't have the resources to keep up with demand and fell by the wayside, replaced by fewer but better-financed mining conglomerates that could weather economic uncertainty. Henry W. Oliver, realizing that he could not rely solely on his own inadequate funds, borrowed a half-million dollars from Carnegie Steel in return for 50 percent ownership of Oliver Iron Mining Company stock. The mining and steel-producing partnership of Oliver-Carnegie

Perhaps the most famous photo location along the Missabe Road is the Boundary Avenue overpass on Proctor Hill, which a "Hill Limestone" job approaches here, on October 13, 1990. In late 2000, the northward track on Proctor Hill was mothballed and all train movements moved to the southward track only. *John Leopard*

grew into one of the more dominant forces in iron mining on the Mesabi and Vermilion ranges and became known simply as "The Oliver."

By the late 1890s, three mining coalitions controlled the flow of ore from northern Minnesota: Rockefeller's Lake Superior Consolidated Mines, the Porter-led syndicate's Minnesota Iron Company/Illinois Steel Company on the Vermilion Range, and the Oliver Iron Mining Company, mining the majority of the Mesabi Range. In December 1896, an alliance between Carnegie, Oliver, and Rockefeller saw the Oliver Iron Mining Company lease all iron ore properties of Lake Superior Consolidated. In addition, James J. Hill, the famed "Empire Builder" of Great Northern Railway fame, was quietly amassing iron ore properties on the western Mesabi Range.

United States Steel

In the late 1890s the big-time operators in the iron and steel industries began to see the advantages of consolidating their holdings of steel mills, raw materials, and water and rail transportation networks. By a complicated series of events, both the Duluth & Iron Range and Duluth, Missabe & Northern came under the control of the newly formed United States Steel Corporation. Incorporated on February 25, 1901, this steel colossus was the first billion-dollar corporation in the

Opposite: Yellowstones could be found working mainline ore trains on both the Iron Range and Missabe divisions after the second order of 10 Yellowstones (M-4 Class Nos. 228–237) arrived in 1943. May 3, 1960, finds No. 231 weighing its train at the Proctor scale house after a southward trip from the Mesabi Range with loads of natural ore. *Bud Bulgrin*

Steaming out of Rainy Junction on June 22, 1956, is Santa Fe–type No. 505 with its 2-10-2 wheel arrangement. The Missabe Road employed a total of sixteen 500-series Santa Fes until they were replaced on mainline assignments by the 2-8-8-4 Yellowstones in the early 1940s. *Bud Bulgrin*

An interesting mix of equipment occupies the whisker tracks at Proctor on this quiet afternoon in 1974. From left to right are Jordan spreader W-200 (which appears to have received a fresh coat of paint), passenger coach No. 33, and, in the background, SD18s 179 and 186 and SD9 No. 158. Built of reinforced concrete in 1917, this 30-stall roundhouse was located at the north end of Proctor Yard. It replaced the original Proctor roundhouse that stood at the south end of the yard when that facility became inadequate for servicing the larger steam power. *Otto P. Dobnick collection*

nation's history. U.S. Steel's assets at the time of its incorporation included 78 blast furnaces and rolling mills; enormous holdings of iron ore, coal, and limestone (the key ingredients of steel); a 112-vessel Great Lakes shipping fleet; and over 1,000 miles of railroad.

U.S. Steel had its origins in the dealings of some of America's most legendary businessmen. The corporation's seed was planted in September 1898, when Judge E. H. Gary, backed by J. P. Morgan, then the controlling force in American banking, organized the Federal Steel Company around the nucleus of their Illinois Steel Company conglomerate. Illinois Steel brought into the fold the iron mines of the Minnesota Iron Company and its transportation holdings of D&IR and the Minnesota Steamship Company. Illinois Steel already owned the Elgin, Joliet & Eastern Railway, a beltline railroad that circled Chicago.

In 1901 an aging Andrew Carnegie was ready to retire from the business world and devote his remaining years to philanthropy. At the behest of Charles Schwab, who

presided over Carnegie's steel-making enterprise, Carnegie sold his vast steel-making holdings—including its subsidiaries, the Bessemer and Lake Erie Railroad and the Pittsburgh Steamship Company—to J. P. Morgan for $492 million, laying the foundation of the United States Steel Corporation. The Pittsburgh Steamship Company had 112 vessels in its fleet, more ships than the U.S. Navy at that time. (The subsidiary was later renamed Pittsburgh Steamship Division on January 1, 1953, and then became known simply as the Pittsburgh Fleet in January 1964. More legal maneuvers saw the fleet emerge as the U.S. Steel Corporation Great Lakes Fleet on July 1, 1967.)

Morgan next sought Lake Superior Consolidated, Rockefeller's mine and transportation network that included the DM&N and the Bessemer Steamship fleet. In mid-March 1901, Rockefeller sold his network to Morgan for $88.5 million.

Continued on page 38

On July 26, 1981, two SD9s grind up the 0.3 percent grade of Saginaw Hill at Grand Lake. To accommodate the mushrooming ore traffic in the early 1900s, the company added a second main track north of Proctor to the Range. By the late 1980s the second main track was no longer needed and was removed between Carson and Fairlane in 1988. ***Robert C. Anderson***

Passenger Service

On April 14, 1957, 4-6-2 Pacific No. 402 fills in for the Budd RDC and steams away from the Two Harbors Depot. The 402 was one of a trio of Pacifics built by Baldwin in 1913 for the DM&N. *Bud Bulgrin*

Alongside its enormous iron ore traffic, the Missabe Road operated a meager network of passenger trains serving the sparse population of the Vermilion and Mesabi ranges.

Passenger service on the Missabe predecessor Duluth & Iron Range was inaugurated on August 11, 1884, with one train per day from Two Harbors to Tower. Over on the Duluth, Missabe & Northern, one-train-per-day operation between Hibbing and Duluth began in 1892, with a second train added in 1902. Through service between Duluth and Winnipeg was promoted in conjunction with the Duluth, Winnipeg & Pacific Railroad, utilizing the DM&N as far north as Virginia. After the DW&P completed its own route into Duluth in 1912, this service was discontinued.

All D&IR and DM&N trains operating out of Duluth used Duluth Union Depot, owned and operated by the Northern Pacific Railway. Commuter train service in Duluth was operated jointly between the D&IR and St. Paul & Duluth

Railway beginning in 1887. Fifteen daily trains were operated between Duluth and nearby Lester Park. The suburban trains were discontinued in 1892 with completion of the parallel Duluth Street Railway, which offered more convenient service.

The early 1920s were the peak period for the passenger trains of the DM&IR predecessor companies. In addition to the DM&N's two daily trains in each direction between Duluth and Hibbing—with a single roundtrip between Duluth and Virginia, plus an Alborn-to-Coleraine connecting train—D&IR operated two daily trains in each direction between Duluth and Ely/Winton via Two Harbors. A connecting train was available from Allen Junction to Virginia, via D&IR's Western Mesaba Branch through Biwabik.

In the years following World War II, people used trains less frequently as improved roads led to competition from buses and automobiles. The trend toward reduced rail service began in 1923 when DM&N trains 5 and 6 between Duluth and Virginia were replaced with an Iron Junction–to–Virginia local train that connected with the Hibbing-to-Duluth runs. The Alborn-to-Coleraine local was discontinued in 1951.

In an attempt to lower costs on passenger-train operations, DM&IR purchased a single Rail Diesel Car (RDC) from the Budd Company. The Model RDC-3, appropriately numbered 1, had 48 coach seats and came equipped with baggage/express and Railway Post Office sections. RDC 1 made its first revenue run from Duluth (Endion) to Ely on January 21, 1953. By this time one pair of Duluth-to-Ely/Winton trains had been dropped and the Duluth terminal shifted from Union Depot to Missabe's own Endion Station, located a mile east of downtown Duluth. Trains 1 and 2 operating between Duluth and Hibbing were discontinued on May 15, 1953.

But the lack of Duluth-to-Hibbing service did not last—on October 6, 1953, the Minnesota Supreme Court upheld an earlier order by the Minnesota Railroad and Warehouse Commission that required the DM&IR to reinstate service between the two cities. The DM&IR immediately appealed the court's ruling, and trains did not operate for the next three years while the case was tied up in litigation. Missabe lost the appeal on November 5, 1956, and was forced to reinstate trains 1 and 2. The RDC assumed this additional run to Hibbing, and coupled with its initial foray to Ely/Winton, operated nearly 400 miles each day. This was a demanding schedule for the company's sole RDC, and 4-6-2 Pacific-type steam locomotives with passenger cars were kept on standby at both Endion and Hibbing in case of mechanical troubles. This reprieve did not last long. Nos. 1 and 2 were allowed to cease operations for a final time on December 31, 1957. Endion-to-Ely trains 5 and 6 continued operating until July 15, 1961, when No. 6 pulled into the Endion Station for the final time, ending all regular scheduled passenger trains on the DM&IR.

Missabe Road RDC-3 No.1 idles in front of the Two Harbors station on June 12, 1960. After the demise of passenger service on the DM&IR, No. 1 was sold to Northern Pacific Railway in March 1963. ***Bud Bulgrin***

The Missabe Road made few trips to the far western end of the Iron Range after 1981, when the last of the natural ore located there had been shipped. In 1992, however, DM&IR began to haul carloads of used railroad ties to an operation based at Bovey that chipped the ties and then trucked them to a nearby paper mill where the chips were burned for fuel. On March 20, 1992, SD9s 129 and 130 power a 43-car train of ties through Keewatin, home of the National Steel Pellet Company, whose plant can be seen in the distance. This movement of used ties lasted a short time and was discontinued in late 1993. *John Leopard*

The new firm also absorbed into its huge grasp the National Steel Company, American Bridge Company, American Sheet Steel Company, American Steel Hoop Company, American Steel & Wire Company, American Tin Plate Company, and the National Tube Company. Each organization brought with it dozens of mills that made everything imaginable out of steel, including beams, barbed wire, rails, pipe, nails, and galvanized sheet steel. Carnegie's Oliver Iron Mining Company and the Minnesota Iron Company retained their identities as separate divisions within U.S. Steel. In its first full year, the corporation controlled over 65 percent of America's steel production, with its annual capacity of finished steel estimated at 7.4 million tons.

In 1901 the Mesabi Range was producing 46 percent of all iron ore in the United States.

Open-hearth-furnace technology improved with the newer Thomas-Gilchrist process that produced a higher-quality steel of a more uniform grade. Blast furnaces no longer required high-grade, low-phosphorous ore, such as the ores produced by ranges in Michigan and Wisconsin and on the Vermilion Range, making the cheaper Mesabi Range ores, which had a higher phosphorous and silica content, more attractive. Most mining development began taking place on the Mesabi Range, and in 1901 the DM&N eclipsed the D&IR in tonnage hauled for the first time.

By 1903 almost two-thirds of mining on the Mesabi Range was controlled by U.S. Steel interests, but independent steel-makers such as Jones & Laughlin Steel Corporation, Wisconsin Steel Company (owned by International Harvester), and Republic Steel Company could also be found mining on the Mesabi Range. Other firms such as Inter-State Iron, Pickands Mather and Company, Hanna Mining, and Cleveland-Cliffs specialized in mining, brokering, and shipping iron ore via the Great Lakes to steel-makers such as Lackawanna Steel Company, Sharon Steel Company, Youngstown Sheet & Tube Company, and Bethlehem Steel Company. In 1907 there were only 11 mines in the world that produced a million tons or better per year—nine of these were located on the Mesabi Range.

Throughout the first decade of the twentieth century, new track construction occurred primarily along the DM&N as the mining frenzy continued on the Mesabi Range. However, a limited amount of track was built by the D&IR when they constructed the Eastern Mesaba Branch from Mesaba to Spring Mine in 1908 and further extended this line in 1910 to mines at Dunka River, 12 miles distant. An 8-mile spur off the Eastern Mesaba Branch to reach timberlands at Ridge was also spiked down at this time. These lines would later prove useful when taconite mining developed in this area during the late 1950s. This period also saw existing D&IR and DM&N lines upgraded with new ties and heavier rail, while many timber trestles were replaced with bridges of all-steel construction.

The Western Mesabi Expands

The ores found on the far western portion of the Mesabi Range contained more impurities than eastern Range ores and were nearly worthless without upgrading. In 1907, the Oliver Iron Mining Company began experimenting with an ore-washing plant at Coleraine. After this introductory plant proved successful, Oliver went on to open a more substantial full-scale washing plant there in April 1910, calling

Missabe SD-M No. 307 shatters the morning silence in the village of Culver as it leads a northward train on October 3, 1991. Unit 307 was originally built by EMD in 1960 as an SD18, then remanufactured at Proctor in 1988. *John Leopard*

it the Trout Lake Concentrator. In simple terms, the ores were washed with water and agitated in sloped tanks where the heavier iron material sank to the bottom and lighter impurities such as sand and silt were carried out the opposite end of the tank by water flow. After washing, the ores assayed to an acceptable level of 57 percent iron content. The pioneering Trout Lake Concentrator became a proving ground for ore-washing technology and more washing plants soon followed. This part of the western Mesabi Range became known as the Canisteo Mining District, and the area prospered after the expanded use of ore-washing and concentrating plants.

Since new mining activity during this period was primarily on the Mesabi's west end, the greatest expansion of rail lines took place in that area. This also answered competition from the Great Northern Railway, which had acquired a small logging railroad, the Duluth, Mississippi River & Northern, to gain access to the Mesabi Range's west end (by 1901 the GN had become the DM&N's principal competitor). Since the DM&N did not yet serve the west end, the Alborn Branch was completed in 1906, extending 55 miles northwest from the mainline at Coleraine Junction, near Alborn, to the developing mines at Coleraine.

Further expansion was required by the increasing output of what became the largest deposit of high-grade ore yet found on the Mesabi Range: the famous Hull-Rust Mine near Hibbing was for many years the largest

Opposite: Early on, the Mesabi Range's natural ore was rich enough to be loaded directly into DM&IR ore cars with no further need for beneficiation. An Oliver Iron Mining Company 700 Class 0-8-0 locomotive, built by the Lima Locomotive Works in 1927, is seen with a cut of DM&IR ore cars in Hibbing's Hull-Rust Mine on October 14, 1942. The 80-foot boom of this electric shovel had a seven-yard dipper capable of handling 15 tons of iron ore in a single bite. *Bud Bulgrin collection*

O. I. M. CO.
707
MISSABE
26022
U20
WI 43600
CAP.
140000

open-pit iron mine in the world. The Hull-Rust group of mines began shipping in 1895 as a small underground operation but within a few years branched out into numerous open-pit mines. Eventually these smaller pits, made up of more than 50 individual mines, began to merge with each other until they collectively became known as the Hull-Rust. The pit became so massive that it was commonly referred to as the "Man-made Grand Canyon of the North." The Hull-Rust grew to become just over 3 miles long, a mile wide, and more than 500 feet deep. It was mined by a number of companies during its tenure and produced over a billion tons of high-grade ore. (Today, this pit continues to grow through taconite mining for the Hibbing Taconite plant.)

The DM&N already served the Hibbing area via the Superior Branch, which met the mainline at Wolf and reached Hibbing in 1893. To handle the torrent of iron ore pouring from the Hull-Rust and other area mines opening at Buhl and Chisholm, a parallel line to the south of the Superior Branch was built in 1905. Called the Shaw Cut-off, this route branched off the Proctor-to-Mountain Iron mainline at Keenan and angled northwest to meet the Superior Branch at Sherwood. The Shaw Cut-off trimmed 5 miles from the ore haul between mines in the Hibbing District and Proctor, eliminated the need to double trains over Macon Hill on the Superior Branch, and avoided the traffic congestion in the Wolf-to-Iron Junction area. But even these track-capacity improvements were not enough. To further relieve congestion on the Superior Branch and improve access to the Hibbing-area mines, the Hull-Rust Short Line was built in 1910. This 18-mile double-track line provided a direct connection between the Hull-Rust pit north of Hibbing and Hull Junction on the Alborn Branch. Traffic warranted adding a second main track to the Alborn Branch between Hull Junction and the mainline at Coleraine Junction.

The Pre-World War I Ore Docks

As ore-tonnage figures mushroomed, it became necessary to expand ore-dock capacity at Two Harbors and Duluth, and work

Deep in the Hull-Rust Mine, a pair of Oliver Iron Mining diesels tugs loaded DM&IR ore cars out of the pit. After the natural ores were gone, portions of the Hull-Rust were mined as a source of taconite ore to supply the pellet plant of the Hibbing Taconite Company. *Iron Range Research Center, Chisholm, Minnesota*

In this view taken in 1967 the rear portion of the Great Lakes Fleet's vessel *William A. Irvin*—and in the distance the vessel *Edmund Fitzgerald*, operated by the Columbia Steamship Company—rest next to Dock No. 6 at Duluth. The *Irvin* is now permanently docked in downtown Duluth, housing a museum since 1986. The *Irvin* was built in 1938 and, at 610 feet in length, had a gross capacity of 8,240 tons. The ill-fated *Fitzgerald* was 730 feet long and launched in 1958. Its hold could could accommodate over 26,000 tons of cargo. *Basgen Photography, author collection*

began in 1904 to extend Duluth's Dock No. 3. Dock No. 1, too low to load the larger vessels that now plied the Great Lakes and with timbers badly in need of replacement, was taken out of service in 1905. The general rebuilding of Dock No. 2, which had been erected in 1896, began that same year. In 1906, crews started construction of Dock No. 4, the last dock built from wood materials in Minnesota. (Wooden docks were later built during World War II in Escanaba, Michigan, by Chicago & North Western and in Port Arthur [Thunder Bay], Ontario, by Canadian National Railway.)

Dock No. 4 was the largest wooden ore dock ever erected, at a length of 2,304 feet and a total capacity of 76,800 tons spread through its 384 pockets. There were 13,782,263 board feet of timber used in its construction—enough material for 1,000 homes. Shortly after the completion of Dock No. 4, however, docks made of wood began to fall from favor as it became apparent they were costly to maintain and posed a fire hazard. The final tally for wooden ore docks was four at Duluth, while five different wooden docks were used at Two Harbors.

Construction of the first steel dock in the United States began at Two Harbors. Completed by the D&IR in 1909, Dock No. 6 was 74 feet high, 920 feet long, and had a capacity of 43,246 tons in its 148 pockets. By 1910,

The vessel *Edwin H. Gott* at the Two Harbors ship-loader on the west side of Dock No. 2 on August 1, 1979. The pellet-storage facility is seen at left, and the Two Harbors roundhouse, back shops, and car-repair facilities are at right. This view, looking west, shows docks Nos. 1, 2, and 6 (right to left). Dock No. 1 sits basically unchanged and was used for conventional railcar unloading and gravity-loading of the ore boats. Dock No. 2 was modified with ship-loader conveyors on its south side, and its north side remained unchanged for gravity loading. Dock No. 6 was out of service at the time of this photo and its rail approach was eliminated when the stockpile area was built. *Basgen Photography, Dan Mackey collection*

timber Dock No. 1 at Two Harbors, falling apart and in need of extensive repairs, was replaced with a new steel dock bearing the same number. Steel Dock No. 1, containing 224 pockets that held 56,000 tons, was completed in 1911. A third steel dock at Two Harbors, Dock No. 2, was completed in 1916 and replaced the wooden dock of the same number. The new No. 2 was the largest dock at Two Harbors, extending 1,368 feet from shore, standing 80 feet above the water surface, and holding 68,400 tons in its 228 pockets. Shortly after steel Dock No. 2 was completed, wooden Docks Nos. 3, 4, and 5 at Two Harbors were completely dismantled.

Erection of the first steel ore dock at Duluth commenced in 1913. Dock No. 5 extended 2,304 feet into the waters of St. Louis Bay and stood 80 feet above the waterline. Its capacity of 115,200 tons easily made it the largest of its kind on the Great Lakes at that time. However, Dock No. 5's status as the largest was not held for long, as completion of a second steel dock closely followed. DM&N Dock No. 6 was opened in 1918. Though 2,304 feet in length (the same as neighboring Dock No. 5), it was 4 feet higher and 5 feet wider, with a whopping 153,600-ton capacity. As of spring 2005, both remained standing, although Dock No.

With the ore cars correctly spotted, dock laborers empty the contents of a car into the pockets below. Some grades of natural ore were difficult to discharge from the cars, requiring workers to manually free the sticky ore with poking poles, a process seen here atop Dock No. 6 at Duluth. Cable harnesses were attached to the workers to prevent them from falling through the bottom of the ore car and into the dock pockets. *Iron Range Research Center, Chisholm, Minnesota*

5 was last used in 1985, when it was shut down due to deteriorating piling conditions and the capability of Dock No. 6 to handle Duluth's entire pellet-shipping tonnage.

In addition to the ore docks at Duluth, an 1,800-foot-long, 600-foot-wide coal-unloading dock was built by the DM&N and placed in service in 1909. Located just east of the ore docks, coal mined in the eastern states arrived here by boat from lower Great Lakes ports.

Continued on page 48

The Duluth Works

Construction of the Minnesota Steel Company began in 1910, and the new integrated steel mill rolled its first billets in December 1915. While being located a mere 70 miles from the world's greatest source of iron ore had its benefits, proximity to the mines was not the only reason for choosing this site near a wide spot in the St. Louis River named Spirit Lake (hence the name of the Duluth, Missabe & Northern subsidiary Spirit Lake Transfer Railway). Most of the mill's production of nails and fencing was destined for the expanding population of the northern Great Plains. In 1930, 540,000 tons of steel were produced in the plant's two blast furnaces.

In 1932 the Minnesota Steel Company was leased to sister U.S. Steel subsidiary American Steel & Wire Company and the plant later became known as U.S. Steel's Duluth Works. At its peak, the works was capable of producing nearly 200,000 miles of barbed wire and 23,000 miles of woven fencing each year. Hundreds of varieties of nails, filling 650,000 kegs holding 100 pounds each, were made annually. During World War II, the plant employed 6,000 workers, making it by far the Missabe Road's largest single industrial customer. The works employed their own fleet of switching locomotives, including 0-4-0T and 0-6-0 steamers, and in later years a small fleet of Baldwin and EMD diesel switchers. A two-stall engine house on the grounds of the works supported the engines.

One of two blast furnaces at the Duluth Works, photographed in 1956. *Basgen Photography, Tom Dorin collection*

Blast-furnace slag, a byproduct from the steelworks, resulted in the construction of a large cement-producing facility adjacent to the Duluth Works, just east of Steelton Yard. The slag, which is formed when limestone reacts with iron ore and coke, contains a number of impurities, such as sulfur, that would make the finished steel brittle. It is, however, a key ingredient in making cement. The cement facility was operated by U.S. Steel and known as Universal-Atlas Cement Division. The slag was transported in pot cars from the furnaces in the steel mill to a dump located near the shore of Spirit Lake where it cooled and hardened. The slag was then reclaimed, crushed, and sent to the U-A plant. In 1958, U-A shipped 34,600 tons of cement in 6,795 cars.

In 1970, steel production tonnage at the Duluth Works reached 970,000 tons with a single furnace. However, all was not well with the American steel industry, as foreign imports gained

One of the main uses for Missabe's fleet of SW9 diesel switchers was in the Steelton Yards and for service to the nearby American Steel & Wire/U.S. Steel Duluth Works and Universal-Atlas cement plant. In 1958, SW9 No. 12 spots DM&IR Class Q hopper cars at the Duluth Works. These cars were nicknamed "battleships" and were used mainly to deliver coal and limestone to the Duluth Works and coal to other online customers. *Basgen Photography, author collection*

AS&W Baldwin VO660 switcher No. 2 works the interchange tracks at Steelton Yard. The AS&W/U.S. Steel Duluth Works diesels wore a black and yellow paint scheme. In the background is the DM&IR Steelton Depot and locomotive sanding tower. *Robert Vierkant, Pete Bonesteel collection*

market share during the 1960s and 1970s and the Duluth Works became a casualty of a contraction of U.S. Steel–owned facilities. Steel production ceased at Duluth in 1971, and the finishing mills followed in 1973. The facility's last operating function was its coal-coking plant, which ceased production in 1979 due to environmental concerns. The Universal-Atlas Cement operations had already come to a halt on January 1, 1976. The razing of the works began in August 1988, leaving behind only a few small buildings and a number of large concrete foundations.

Much of the coal was used in DM&N steam locomotives and stationary boilers, as well as being shipped to various Oliver Iron Mining properties on the Iron Range. The coal dock took on a greater role after the completion of the Minnesota Steel Company's mill in far western Duluth in 1915—eastern coal was used to feed that new steel mill's battery of coke ovens.

The Spirit Lake and Interstate Transfer Railways

In 1907 the DM&N formed two connecting terminal railroad companies in the Twin Ports of Duluth and Superior, Wisconsin, in preparation for serving a planned steel mill in west Duluth. The first was the Spirit Lake Transfer Railway, built primarily to haul iron ore to, and finished product from, the Minnesota

An eastward Steelton Switch run vaults across the St. Louis River via the 1,889-foot-long Oliver Bridge in late October 1985. This length includes a 300-foot-long swing span, and it is at this point that the river marks the boundary between Minnesota and Wisconsin. Visible between the bridge's twin decks are the idled structures of the Duluth Works steel mill. *Otto P. Dobnick*

Steel Company's plant that began construction in 1910. The 11-mile route connected with the DM&N mainline at Adolph, just north of Proctor Yard, then dropped steeply down the Laurentian Shield on what the railroad alternately called Nevada or Steelton Hill. This was the same escarpment traversed by the Proctor Hill Line while en route to the Duluth ore docks located 5 miles to the northeast.

At the foot of the grade was Steelton Yard in Duluth's Gary neighborhood, which soon became a beehive of activity with the primary purpose of supporting the nearby steel mill. A connection with Northern Pacific's subsidiary, Duluth Transfer Railway, and its line from the west-end neighborhood of Duluth, would later allow the Duluth, Missabe & Iron Range (via trackage rights) to bring eastern-mined coal and limestone to the plant. These materials were brought into Duluth by lake boats.

The second of the DM&N subsidiary roads was the Interstate Transfer Railway. Its main function was to connect with the major railroads serving Superior, Wisconsin. To reach Superior, the 1,889 foot long, two deck Oliver Bridge was built across the St. Louis River between Steelton and Oliver, Wisconsin. The top deck was for railroad

Missabe Road SD9s 153 and 157 lead a train of natural ore through the S-curve on the approach trestle to Dock No. 5 on May 13, 1970. Dock No. 5 remains standing to this day but has not seen use since 1985 due to the deteriorated conditions of its pilings and the ability of Dock No. 6 to handle all of Duluth's ore-shipping needs. ***J. David Ingles***

Yellowstone No. 230 backs onto the 128-foot-long turntable at Proctor in early 1960. At the time these large engines were delivered, the turntable and roundhouse stall lengths could not handle their longer wheelbase. At Proctor, the turntable bridge was increased from 100 to 128 feet, and 10 longer stalls were added to the roundhouse. Similar problems existed at Two Harbors, where a new eight-stall concrete engine house was built because the existing 30-stall roundhouse and turntable were too small to accommodate the giant articulated engines. *Bud Bulgrin*

use, the bottom for vehicle and pedestrian traffic. Once across the river, the Interstate Transfer's rails ran east to a connection with the Chicago, St. Paul, Minneapolis & Omaha at Itasca, Wisconsin, and along the way intercepted rails of the Northern Pacific, Great Northern, Soo Line, and Duluth, South Shore & Atlantic. Construction of the Spirit Lake and the Interstate Transfer was completed by 1915 in conjunction with the completion of the steel mill; both of these companies were "paper" subsidiaries and not operating railroads.

The next expansion took place while the DM&N and D&IR were under control of the United States Railway Administration during World War I. The 15-mile-long Wales Branch was built in 1917 to reach logging camps north of Two Harbors. Four sizeable lumbering operations were initially served along the Wales Branch, including a sawmill at the end of the line at Whyte.

Ore traffic steadily increased in the years before, during, and after World War I. The combined tonnage figure for both the DM&N and D&IR in 1916 was 33,334,925, an amount not exceeded until World War II. During these peak periods, as many as fifty 65-car road trains could be found operating across the system. A trainload of ore was brought down Proctor Hill to the ore docks as frequently as every 15 minutes. At Proctor, the year 1917 saw the completion of a new 30-stall roundhouse built of reinforced concrete, with a new 100-foot-long turntable to feed it.

After the war, in 1920, U.S. Steel's Oliver Iron Mining Division operated 128 different mines. That same year, smaller companies like Jones & Laughlin worked 15 mines, Pickands Mather had 29, Republic Iron and Steel 10, Cleveland-Cliffs 9, and Hanna Mining 33. Production levels for iron ore remained steady during the 1920s, hovering in the low 20-million-ton range. By 1924, there were 36 ore-washing and screening plants operating on the iron ranges.

The Great Depression sparked in October 1929, however, stifling the steel-making and iron-mining industries, and soon blast furnaces in every steel-producing region of the country sat idle. Total tonnage on both railroads plummeted to 1,458,711 in 1932, less than that hauled in 1893 when the DM&N first began operating their own docks at Duluth. In 1932, no solid ore trains ran—all of the ore was handled in local freights. Helping to ease the financial pain somewhat was the lease of the D&IR to the corporately stronger DM&N. This first major step in the unification of the two roads became effective on January 10, 1930. The consolidation provided considerable economies by eliminating duplicate facilities and bringing about the joint use of equipment. Ore traffic rebounded sharply in 1933 to just over 9 million tons, but fluctuated greatly throughout the 1930s.

On March 17, 1992, SD9 No. 170 leads a trainload of Fairlane-produced pellets past the depot at Saginaw. Southward trains at this point are digging in for a 0.3 percent grade that tops out just east of the depot. This is the ruling grade for loaded trains on the Missabe Division mainline. ***John Leopard***

In February 1970, SD18 No. 180 was adorned in Missabe's new arrowhead paint scheme reflecting the arrowhead shape of northeastern Minnesota on a map. In two-main track territory near Keenan on May 14, 1978, a southward loaded T-Bird run behind SD18 No. 185 meets a northbound train led by SD9 No. 166, still dressed in Missabe's original paint scheme. *Robert C. Anderson*

CHAPTER THREE

TWO RAILROADS BECOME ONE

Corporate maneuvers leading to the direct consolidation of the Duluth & Iron Range and Duluth, Missabe & Northern began on July 1, 1937, when the DM&N and the Spirit Lake Transfer Railway were merged to form the Duluth, Missabe & Iron Range Railway Company. Next, the D&IR and the Interstate Transfer Railway were acquired by the DM&IR on March 21, 1938, with dissolution of the D&IR and Interstate Transfer as corporations coming just a few months later. (The DM&IR would remain a subsidiary of U.S. Steel until it was partially

On an August 1991 afternoon, an empty train en route to Minntac negotiates the north leg of the wye at Iron Junction while leaving the Biwabik Branch and entering the Missabe Division mainline toward Minntac. Iron Junction was Missabe's busiest location in terms of train movements, resulting in one of the company's first applications of CTC signaling, put in service through this area in 1943. *John Leopard*

purchased by Blackstone Capital Partners in 1988.) Two operating divisions were formed following the creation of the DM&IR in 1938. Generally speaking, the Missabe Division was composed of former DM&N lines, while the old D&IR routes constituted the Iron Range Division. The Spirit Lake and Interstate Transfer Railways became the Spirit Lake and the Interstate branches of the Missabe Division.

With the development of continuous-rolled wide-strip steel in the 1930s, sheet steel became commonly available for such things as autos and appliances. These new markets for steel created yet more demand for iron ore. In 1939, "Missabe Road" ore tonnage doubled over the previous year to 18.6 million tons, signaling the long-awaited recovery. In 1941, tonnage climbed to a staggering 37 million tons, as the United States and its allies geared up to fight Germany, Italy, and Japan. Arrival of the first eight of Missabe's famed 2-8-8-4 Yellowstone locomotives from the Baldwin Locomotive Works in 1941, plus 1,500 new 70-ton-capacity ore cars, enabled the Missabe to move 44,788,199 tons of ore that year, the Missabe Road's best year up to that time.

Production levels at the mines continued to rise with the wartime demands. The largest mine of them all, the Hull-Rust at Hibbing,

Opposite: In addition to modifications at locomotive servicing facilities to accommodate the larger Yellowstones, improvements to track structure were needed, including heavier 115-pound rail. In double-track territory, track centers on tight curves were increased to allow the long boilers of the articulated Yellowstones to clear train movements on adjacent tracks. One of Missabe's fabled Yellowstones arrives in Proctor with a trainload of natural ore on June 6, 1959. *Robert C. Anderson*

Santa Fe–type No. 504 switches a cut of cabooses at Proctor on May 17, 1956. One of the Missabe's Santa Fes, No. 506, was donated to the National Railroad Museum in Green Bay, Wisconsin, in 1962. *Robert C. Anderson*

dug out 12 million tons in 1944. To safely handle more trains, the Missabe installed 5 miles of double-track Centralized Traffic Control (CTC) signaling and 6 miles of single-track CTC in 1943. The territory protected by CTC included junctions at Keenan, Iron Junction, and Wolf on the Missabe Division mainline, and switches at Sparta and Spruce on the Biwabik Branch. At the time, up to 90 train movements a day were governed by the new signal system in this territory. Over time, CTC signaling expanded to nearly all mainline trackage across the Iron Range.

Postwar Growth and Decline

In all, Minnesota's three iron ranges supplied 339 million tons of iron ore during World War II. At the end of the war, however, the high-grade reserves were nearing exhaustion, so the mining companies turned to the soft, intermediate, and low-grade ores still remaining. Additional processing plants were built to beneficiate these lower-quality ores. Various methods and machinery were used, and by 1958 more than 70 different ore-processing

The Wales Branch was built in 1917 to aid in harvesting the area's huge stands of virgin timber. When these lands had been cleared, the second-growth timber proved undesirable to the lumbering companies. However, consumer demand for paper products led to a renewed interest in these lands for pulpwood harvesting, and the line was extended to Forest Center in 1948. In 1961, Alco RSD15s 54 and 55 pick up a cut of flatcars heavily loaded with pulpwood at Isabella. ***Basgen Photography, author collection***

Yellowstone No. 235 approaches the scales at Proctor on May 3, 1960. Not only was everything about these locomotives big, but each was accompanied by an equally impressive 4-10-0 pedestal-type "centipede" coal tender. With Missabe's classic "wing" logo stretching its entire length, each of these tenders hauled up to 26 tons of coal and 25,000 gallons of water. Trailing the tender is ore car No. 27770, one of more than 9,800 70-ton ore cars owned by the company in 1960. *Bud Bulgrin*

and washing plants had been built across the Mesabi Range to make ores more attractive to steel makers. (The Great Northern Railway, which was now hauling nearly one-third of the Mesabi Range's iron ore production, served some of these plants.) By 1961, shipments of iron concentrates on the DM&IR exceeded those of direct-shipping natural ores.

Iron ore traffic was not the only traffic on the upswing for the DM&IR: after World War II, consumer demand for paper products exploded. In the 1940s the U.S. Forest Service opened up a portion of the Superior National Forest for selective timber cutting, and the Tomahawk Timber Company acquired the rights to harvest some 150,000 acres of these timberlands. This resulted in a 32-mile-long extension of the Wales Branch from Whyte to Forest Center, where the Tomahawk Timber Company built a large logging camp. Track was laid during 1947 and 1948 with great difficulty, as much of the line traversed unstable swampy areas. For the first six years of the extension's operation, an average of 5,000 carloads of pulpwood were handled each year, a considerable amount of which was sent to paper mills in Cloquet, Minnesota, and central Wisconsin.

The Korean War, and a surging demand for consumer goods, sent the Missabe's tonnage for 1953 to a new record—49,317,625 tons. Then, in the late 1950s, Minnesota's iron ore production slumped badly. This wasn't due to problems in the U.S. economy—American steel makers were as busy as they'd ever been in a nonwar economy. Rather, a number of factors were beginning to stack up against Minnesota's iron-mining industry; namely, the Mesabi Range was running out of the abundant and easy-to-mine

New SD9s 160 and 165 idle in front of the diesel shop on May 29, 1959. These units were part of the last order of that model, Nos. 159 through 174. All of the fuel tanks on Missabe's SD9 fleet were of the small 1,200-gallon variety, since DM&IR's road hauls were short and fueling facilities were always close by. Beneath the frame and in front of the small fuel tanks the DM&IR attached 6 tons of steel plates to increase the weight of the units to 387,000 pounds. *Bud Bulgrin*

natural ore. The dark days of the early 1960s found mining costs ratcheting upward as the pits ran deeper and the mines treated what lower-grade ores remained. In addition, newly found deposits of high-grade ore from overseas sources like Venezuela, Peru, and Brazil, as well as from Labrador, Canada, began to displace Minnesota ore in American blast furnaces. These imports were made cost-effective by huge new oceangoing ore ships up to five times bigger than most Great Lakes ore boats.

The Missabe Road began to dieselize road operations during these trying times with an initial purchase of 10 Electro-Motive Division (EMD) SD9 locomotives. These 1,750-horsepower units were placed in service

The engineer has just snagged his train orders from the fork in front of the joint BN/DM&IR Marble-Calumet depot on July 4, 1977. This westbound train of empty ore cars is destined for the High Grade Yard near Bovey. The DM&IR gained trackage rights over the GN through here when its own parallel line to the north was removed in the 1920s as a result of expanded mining activities. *Robert C. Anderson*

upon the opening of the 1956 ore-hauling season. These road engines had been preceded in 1953 by EMD SW9 diesel locomotives used in switching and transfer service. Dieselization was largely completed in 1960 with the last steam-powered ore train running on July 5, 1960, headed by Yellowstone No. 222. By that point, ore-traffic figures were hovering around 19 million tons per year, and total route mileage operated by the DM&IR was just over 550.

The natural ore deposits near Hibbing and the Canisteo District were nearing exhaustion by the end of the 1950s, resulting in a drop in train traffic on the western Mesabi Range. In 1959 a proposal was drawn up between the DM&IR and Great Northern to consolidate trackage on the western Mesabi. The Interstate Commerce Commission (ICC) approved the plan on March 25, 1960, permitting GN to operate trains between Kelly Lake (GN's main base for Mesabi Range operations) and Virginia by routing over DM&IR track between Emmert (just east of Hibbing) and Virginia via Keenan and Wolf. In exchange, GN would abandon its track between Virginia and Emmert, and DM&IR trains used GN rails west from Emmert through Hibbing and Nashwauk to Holman Junction. GN had previously garnered trackage rights over the DM&IR between Holman Junction and Coleraine due to expanded mining activities at the Canisteo Mine.

Management studies under way in 1961 even went so far as to recommend a joint DM&IR/GN ore-blending yard and plant that would allow the shutdown of either or both of the DM&IR docks at Duluth or the GN docks at Allouez (Superior), Wisconsin. Other 1961 studies mentioned in management reports of that era suggested options for abandoning the Missabe Division mainline north of Proctor and routing all ore traffic through the dock at Two Harbors. Annual tonnage levels ranging from 15 to 25 million were used as a basis for these studies. For the most part, though, nothing ever came of these drastic proposals.

Changes were also affecting the eastern edge of the system. With the closing of the

On the first day of spring 1992, SD9s 129 and 130 make the trestle timbers creak while leading a train of used railroad ties on BN trackage near Calumet. After the natural ore deposits on the west end of the Mesabi Range were exhausted, there was little reason for DM&IR trains to travel west of Hibbing, so most of the railroad's west-end track was abandoned in favor of trackage rights over this former Great Northern line. In 1994 BN replaced this large wooden trestle with a more modern steel-and-concrete structure. In February 2004, a portion of this line still owned by the DM&IR near Bovey was taken out of service due to high groundwater swelling from the dormant Canisteo Mine. BNSF taconite trains and unit coal trains destined for Keenan (Laskin power plant) had to be rerouted over other BNSF lines. *John Leopard*

Pioneer Mine at Ely in 1967, there were no longer any active mines on the Vermilion Range. While there was ore left to be dug, it was simply too expensive for the deep underground mines to continue extracting it. The Soudan Mine shaft extended down to 2,400 feet, making it the deepest in the state. There were later shipments from stockpiles, but for the most part, mining activity on the Vermilion Range was done. More than 100 million tons of iron ore had been mined from the Vermilion, and the related drop in tonnage due

to these closures culminated in the mothballing of the ore docks at Two Harbors in 1963; they would not reopen until taconite plants came online in 1966.

Taking on Taconite

Taconite is the most abundant form of iron-bearing rock on the Mesabi Range. When Minnesota state geologist N. H. Winchell explored the Mesabi Range in the early 1880s, he called the extensive body of pre-Cambrian rock "Taconic Strata" in his reports, borrowing the name from the Taconic Mountains of Massachusetts, where similar-looking rock had been found many years prior. The name was appropriate; in certain Native American languages, "taconite" means "wild land" or "forest wilderness."

For years, mining companies bypassed the taconite rock on the Mesabi Range because of its low iron content, great hardness, and high abrasiveness. Experiments in refining taconite

On March 17, 1992, SD9 No.130 bends around the connecting track between the DM&IR and DW&P lines at Shelton Junction with 20 loads of Minorca-produced pellets. The train is coming off the DW&P mainline and heading on to the DM&IR Virginia Branch. ***John Leopard***

ore were conducted by the University of Minnesota on the Mesabi as early as 1913, in which they attempted to crush and then separate the iron particles from the hard taconite rock by mechanical, chemical, and electrical means. Another group conducted further tests between 1915 and 1920 and felt confident enough in their findings to proceed with the construction of the world's first commercial taconite-processing plant, located near Babbitt. When production began on June 21, 1922, the Mesabi Iron Company was served by a spur of the Duluth & Iron Range. The Babbitt facility processed 350 to 400 tons of high-grade concentrated ore per day. While the product was deemed a success, the processing technology wasn't mature enough and it could not compete with the lower cost of Mesabi Range natural ore. The plant ceased operations in June 1924.

The University of Minnesota and other mining and steel company interests continued experiments throughout the 1930s and 1940s. These enterprises knew that the natural ore deposits would not last forever and stepped up their efforts to find workable methods of extracting iron from taconite rock. Their research eventually proved that a profitable means of liberating iron particles embedded in taconite rock could be accomplished on a large commercial scale. While different companies use a variety of methods and equipment, the principles are the same.

The taconite rock is mined by drilling and blasting, then is shipped to a processing plant where a series of crushers reduce the ore to uniform 3/4-inch pebbles. This fine ore is pulverized into a powderlike consistency at a grinding mill, where it is fed into rotating horizontal drums and tumbled with 2- to 5-inch-diameter steel balls or steel rods measuring about 20 feet long and 4 inches in diameter. The ore is now fine enough that the iron particles can be separated from the waste rock by using strong magnets. The resulting iron particles are called "concentrate." Nonmagnetic sands left over from the grinding process are washed away with water. This waste material is referred to as "tailings." Filters then draw water away from the iron concentrate, leaving only about 10 percent moisture. At this stage, the iron-bearing material is known as "filter cake" and has a 60 to 65 percent iron content.

Separating the iron particles from the host rock was one problem; putting them together in a form fit for blast furnace consumption was another. Spherical pellets were deemed the answer. Bentonite clay is added to the filter cake, which is conveyed to balling drums, where the material rolls around and around until formed into marble-sized pellets that are hardened in a long rotary or flat-grate kiln at a temperature of 2,400 degrees Fahrenheit. This makes the pellets extremely hard so that they can withstand handling and shipment.

Taconite pellets have several qualities that give them advantages over natural ore. The consistency of natural ore is very similar to that of dirt, and it tends to "cake up" in steel mill blast furnaces. The uniform pellets not only have a favorable chemical content, but outperform natural ore once inside the furnace. The spherical pellets allow hot furnace gases to reach every particle equally, which allows them to reduce more quickly into molten iron, thus increasing production rates.

Erie Mining and Reserve Mining

While lab experiments continued, various interests drilled and searched for high-grade taconite formations, which tended to be found in the eastern half of the Mesabi Range. Erie Mining Company (EMCo) was formed in 1940 on a shared-percentage basis by three steel-producing companies: Bethlehem Steel, Youngstown Sheet & Tube, and Interlake Iron and Steel Company. The Steel Company of Canada (Stelco) came aboard in 1952. The iron-mining and shipping firm of Pickands

Taconite-processing plants are massive, complex installations. This interior view of a grinding mill illustrates where the ore is ground to the fineness of flour. *Basgen Photography, author collection*

The DM&IR was not the only railroad on the Mesabi Range to operate a collection of classic diesel locomotives. Erie Mining, and later LTV Steel Mining Company, relied on a fleet of F9 locomotives on its mainline pellet trains, along with an assortment of Alco, EMD, and Baldwin products in mine-run and switching use. Reserve Mining, later Cyprus Northshore, and most recently Northshore Mining, used an interesting collection of EMD-built SD9, SD18, SD28, and SD38-2 diesels to power its mainline crude ore runs. On August 8, 1991, loaded trains of LTV and Cyprus Northshore Mining are seen south of Babbitt, where the mainlines of both routes cross. *John Leopard*

Mather & Company was the managing agent for these companies.

Pickands Mather established a laboratory on the western Mesabi Range in Hibbing in 1942 to test its ideas for removing impurities from taconite ore. In 1946, satisfied with its Hibbing experiments, Erie Mining began construction of a preliminary taconite-processing plant on the eastern Mesabi near Aurora. The facility, called Pretac, was the first to use commercial-sized, as opposed to laboratory, equipment in testing taconite beneficiating processes. With an annual production rate of 200,000 tons of ore concentrate, it was much larger than the old Babbitt facility of the ill-fated Mesabi Iron Company in the 1920s. Pretac began its testing in July 1948.

Not far behind Erie Mining was another consortium that called itself the Reserve Mining Company. Its research was conducted at the old Mesabi Iron Company site near Babbitt. Iron-mining and shipping merchant Oglebay Norton & Company incorporated Reserve

The construction of Erie Mining's pellet plant at Hoyt Lakes benefited the DM&IR, which delivered construction supplies and, after the Erie plant was completed, continued to haul in raw materials used in pellet production. On May 23, 1996, the Miscellaneous Road Freight (MRF) positions cars at the interchange tracks while an LTV crude-ore mine-run train, powered by an Alco RS11/EMD GP38 combination, passes high above en route to the plant's crusher. *Doug Buell*

Mining in 1939 as the agent for four large steelmaking companies: American Rolling Mill Company (later Armco), Cleveland-Cliffs Iron Company, Republic Steel, and Wheeling-Pittsburgh. At about the same time Erie was perfecting its process at the Pretac plant, Reserve was also developing machinery necessary to crush, screen, concentrate, and pelletize taconite rock. Erie's and Reserve's findings resulted in the first two large-scale investments in the processing of Minnesota taconite.

Reserve Mining moved first, building a large commercial-scale taconite-processing facility, located along the shore of Lake Superior at Silver Bay, which began production in 1955. The ore processed there was mined near Babbitt, and the operation required a brand-new railroad to haul crude ore through 47 miles of wilderness between the mine and processing plant. By 1961 the Reserve facility at Silver Bay was capable of producing nine million tons of pellets annually. The DM&IR benefited by hauling the construction materials used to build the Reserve facilities. The Reserve railroad passed over the Missabe's

In 1952, the DM&IR received 20 of the first production steel wide-vision cabooses in the country. Numbered C-200 through C-219, these cabooses were constructed by the International Car Company. Caboose C-203 is about to duck under the DW&P mainline at Munger on June 1, 1974, while bringing up the rear of a northward empty train. *Tom Murray*

Wales Branch at a location named Norshor Junction, where an interchange track was spiked down. The DM&IR continued to benefit after Reserve's construction was complete by handling inbound shipments of bentonite clay, grinding rods and balls, and other materials used by Reserve.

Using the lessons learned at its Pretac plant, Erie Mining began building the second full-scale Mesabi Range taconite-processing operation in 1954. Differing from Reserve, Erie chose to build its pelletizing plant inland from Lake Superior, next to its ore reserves near Mesaba. Erie also built a 72-mile rail line to haul pellets to a new ore dock on Lake Superior. Initially, the Erie plant was capable of producing 7.5 million tons of pellets each year, but a project completed in 1967 increased this output to 10.3 million tons annually. Much like Reserve Mining, Erie proved to be a valuable traffic source for the DM&IR, both during Erie's construction and afterward; interchange tracks were located along the line to Ely, at a location called Hinsdale, 5 miles north of Allen Junction.

United States Steel and Taconite

Due to its affiliation with Carnegie, the Oliver Iron Mining Company had become a division of U.S. Steel after the complicated proceedings that formed the corporation in 1901. Because it was the Oliver's responsibility to make sure there were sufficient ore reserves to supply the furnaces of parent U.S. Steel, they watched the developments of the Erie and Reserve projects with great interest.

In 1944, Oliver established an experimental laboratory in West Duluth to study taconite and began acquiring land between Virginia and Buhl containing a taconite formation with consistent-quality iron content. Based on research conducted in their laboratory, the

Loading tracks were constantly shifted and relocated as the benches of ore on which they were laid were mined. In this corner of the Mountain Iron Mine pit, Oliver Iron Mining steam locomotive No. 603 is closely followed by an on-track crane that is in the process of shifting track to another location. It was at this mine that the Merritt brothers first discovered ore on the Mesabi Range in 1892. *Bud Bulgrin collection*

Oliver Iron Ore Division—the name change occurred in 1951—constructed the Pilotac (*Pilo*t *Ta*conite *C*oncentrator) test plant on the deposit west of Virginia. Pilotac opened in 1953 and was capable of producing around 500,000 tons of concentrate per year. The goals of Pilotac were to perfect the crushing and concentrating methods, as well as the machinery that would later be duplicated on a much larger commercial scale at the Minntac facility.

To process the concentrated iron fines produced at Pilotac into a usable product for steel mills, Oliver built the Extaca (*Ex*perimental *Ta*conite *A*gglomerator) plant. Agglomeration is defined as gathering a large number of smaller particles, in this case iron, into a larger mass, such as a taconite pellet, sufficiently strong enough to withstand rough handling, such as loading into railcars and lake boats.

Extaca was completed at roughly the same time as Pilotac and was located on the site of Oliver's massive Rouchleau ore-crushing and screening facility south of Virginia. Extaca experimented with large equipment such as a nodulizing kiln and traveling grate system used for *sintering* the concentrate. In the sintering process, pulverized damp ore is mixed with fine coal. At Extaca, the mixture was spread evenly on a grate system and the surface ignited, causing the particles to fuse together into a strong porous mass that was crushed into a gravel-like consistency.

The iron fines were shipped between Pilotac and Extaca via the DM&IR, which modified a small fleet of ore cars for this service. However, by the time Minntac was constructed, newer agglomerating methods, namely pelletizing,

At the Sherman Mine between the towns of Buhl and Chisholm, a shovel made by Bucyrus-Erie scoops natural ore for loading into a waiting train of side-dump cars. The locomotive spotting the cars is a Baldwin VO1000 switcher lettered for the Oliver Iron Mining Division of U.S. Steel. ***Iron Range Historical Society, Gilbert, Minnesota***

Rouchleau Plant, Virginia, Minn.

Above: On a late summer afternoon, SD18 No. 179 switches at the Rainy Junction Yard in this postcard view. The structure on the left is the Rouchleau ore crusher; visible behind the trestle is a portion of the Extaca plant that used a nodulizing kiln and a traveling grate to sinter taconite concentrate shipped by rail from the nearby Pilotac plant. *Pete Bonesteel collection*

Left: Oliver Iron Mining Company dieselized in the 1940s with new Alco and Baldwin switchers replacing a steam locomotive fleet made up mainly of heavy 0-8-0 switchers. On May 13, 1978, Oliver's Baldwin Model DS4-4-1000 No. 932 positions DM&IR ore cars at the Sherman Mine for loading. *Steve Glischinski*

had been developed and much of the equipment and processes tested at Extaca were not used at Minntac. Extaca was shut down in the 1960s just prior to the opening of the Minntac plant. Then, in 1963, the Oliver name disappeared altogether when corporate reshuffling saw the mining division resurface under the guise of USS Minnesota Ore Operations.

Taconite Amendment

The opening of the Reserve Mining and Erie Mining plants provided some of the few

Brake-shoe smoke emanates from a loaded taconite train braking through the Collingwood interlocking plant at Duluth on October 13, 1990. This dispatcher-controlled interlocking governs movements to the approach tracks, which access the ore docks and a junction with the line to Missabe Junction and downtown Duluth. The unique signal bridge supported signals that governed northward train movements; it was removed in the early 1990s. *John Leopard*

highlights for the Iron Range in the late 1950s and early 1960s. In the early 1960s economic hardship loomed and production of natural ore was at the lowest level since the Great Depression. The slow growth of the taconite industry was disappointing, as the capital requirements were substantial and the State of Minnesota was unable to offer the taconite plants long-term guarantees on the amount of taxes they would have to pay to operate.

A major stumbling block for companies looking to invest in taconite plants was Minnesota's state government tax on ore reserves. The mining companies paid an *ad valorem* ("in proportion to the value") tax on unmined natural ore. To mining firms, the most objectionable feature of this was that every ton of ore in the ground was taxed each year until it was mined and shipped out. Minnesota had a reputation of taxing iron ore operations at an unprecedented rate.

In pretaconite times, the mining companies could afford the high tax rates because mining the soft, high-grade hematite was cheap, easy, and very profitable. Plus, ore was not "discovered" on the small deposits being

mined until immediately before mining. Taconite was everywhere on the Mesabi. If billions of tons of this rock were suddenly reclassified as minable reserves, some of which might not be mined for 50 or more years, the cost of paying these taxes would become prohibitive. In the taconite era, with its high capital costs, this risk was not acceptable to the mining companies.

A change to these tax laws in 1941 spurred the Erie and Reserve projects by replacing the *ad valorem* tax on taconite with a production tax, charging the companies a set amount for each ton shipped. Still, more permanent legislation was sought—the state legislature could just as easily change back the tax laws once the industry was established. By the early 1960s it was clear that the mining companies were not going to risk investing large sums in taconite plants unless the state constitution was amended to limit taxes on taconite-processing operations to amounts similar to other manufacturing operations in the state. This feat was accomplished on November 3, 1964, after an intensive lobbying effort convinced Minnesota's citizens to

A fraction of the sprawling Fairlane pellet plant is seen in this February 27, 1991, view of a train being loaded with taconite pellets. Opened in the fall of 1965, Fairlane was the first full-scale taconite-processing facility served by the Missabe Road. *John Leopard*

overwhelmingly pass what became known as the "Taconite Amendment," assuring a future for Minnesota's iron-mining industry. What the steel and mining companies received for their efforts was a 25-year shift to a production tax based on the amount of taconite actually processed and shipped. Though the Taconite Amendment expired in 1989, the primary way of taxing the iron-mining industry in Minnesota remains the production tax.

Eveleth Taconite Company

The Ford Motor Company and Oglebay Norton & Company, confident enough in the passage of the impending tax legislation to proceed with plans for a taconite-processing facility, incorporated the Eveleth Taconite Company in 1963. This would be the first facility of its kind to be served by the DM&IR. Ford's 85 percent ownership of Eveleth Taconite was reflected in its names for the mine, Thunderbird, and the pellet plant, Fairlane, both prominent models in Ford's automobile line. The Fairlane plant was originally capable of turning out 1.6 million tons of pellets annually, all of them destined for Ford's River Rouge steel-making complex near Detroit, Michigan. This reflected Ford's belief in a totally integrated approach to vehicle manufacturing. Fairlane's first pellets were produced in December 1965, sent to Duluth via the DM&IR, and

Missabe SD38DC No. 222, a former EJ&E unit, brings the first of 83 cars through the Thunderbird north loadout on May 12, 2003. Once loaded, the train will depart for the pellet plant at Fairlane, 10 miles away. A similar loading facility was utilized at the Thunderbird south mine until it was closed in 1992. *David C. Schauer*

A light snow powders the ground on February 14, 1987, as a single SD-M and two SD38s lead a train into the Fairlane pellet plant for loading. In the background is a pile of raw taconite ore known as a surge pile. If the crusher bins are full, excess crude ore is transported to this pile by the high-level conveyor seen above the train. It is reclaimed underneath the pile and conveyed back to the fine crusher as needed by the inclined conveyor coming out of the ground. A surge pile is maintained in the event that the flow of coarse ore from the mine to the plant is interrupted by weather or mechanical failure. *Robert C. Anderson*

immediately sent to stockpile to await the opening of the Great Lakes shipping season in April 1966. An expansion program concluded in 1968 brought plant capacity up to 2.3 million tons annually.

The Thunderbird Mine, near Eveleth, and the pellet plant, 10 miles to the south at Forbes, were connected by the DM&IR. The pellet plant was so located in order to tap the St. Louis River for the large amounts of water it

needed in its pelletizing process. DM&IR hauled the firm's crude ore using trains popularly known as "T-Birds," which operated in a conveyor belt-like fashion between loading pockets at the mine areas (each equipped with a runaround track) and a loop unloading track at the pellet plant. In good economic times the T-Birds ran around the clock, seven days a week, with each crew making two roundtrips per eight-hour shift. Two crews were on duty at any given time, scheduled so that one was loading at the mine while the other was unloading at the plant.

A loading chute dips into the hold of the vessel *Edmund Fitzgerald* to deposit a load of taconite pellets at Dock No. 6 in Duluth in 1967. The cargo hatches—24 feet on center, the same length as an ore car—and every other dock chute—12 feet on center—are lowered at a given time to load a ship. Once the first set of pockets is emptied, the ship is inched forward to line up with another set of loaded pockets. *Basgen Photography, author collection*

An interesting note is that Eveleth Taconite's first pellet shipment was loaded aboard the ill-fated Great Lakes steamer *Edmund Fitzgerald* on April 8, 1966. Nine years later the boat sank into the depths of Lake Superior on a stormy November 10, 1975, resulting in the loss of all 29 crew members.

Minntac Pellet Plant

Armed with the knowledge gained at the Pilotac and Extaca research projects, and with the new taxation laws, U.S. Steel felt the time was right to enter into the world of taconite pellet production. As the first pellets were being baked at neighboring Eveleth Taconite, construction was already under way on U.S. Steel's Minntac Pellet Plant. This installation was located a few miles northwest of Virginia, not far from the place where the Merritts had discovered natural ore on the Mesabi Range [illegible] years earlier. Minntac hauled its first trainload of pellets in October 1967, with

Continued on page 78

Minntac Mining Railroad

Until the 1930s, ore was transported from most Minnesota open-pit iron mines by privately owned mine railroads. When Euclid and Mack introduced early production trucks suitable for mining duty in 1937, these trucks quickly displaced rail haulage in most mines not owned by U.S. Steel. The trucks proved more maneuverable than trains and capable of climbing steeper grades. The development of conveyor belts further added to the demise of pit rails.

Once-extensive steam and electric pit-rail operations were reduced to overland transfers between pit edges and plants at several operations, but were eliminated altogether at most (plants built in the 1960s and 1970s used trucks from the start). The lone non–U.S. Steel exception was the Erie Mining Company, where rail haulage was deemed economical because of the still relatively small trucks available in the 1950s and problems that arose keeping tires on in the hard, sharp taconite rock. Erie started rail operations with a new fleet of Alco and Baldwin diesels in 1957. Direct loading of trains in the Erie pit was phased out in the 1970s, but transfer of ore by rail from the pits to the plant continued until the plant closed down in January 2001.

USS continued rail haulage in the large natural ore mines of all three mining districts on the Mesabi through the 1960s. As Minntac was developed, management decided to utilize rail haulage in the pit, starting mainly with surplus equipment from the natural ore operations.

From its beginning, Minntac utilized a private standard gauge railroad to move crude taconite ore to the coarse crushers. In its first years the crude-ore trains were required to travel just 2 to 3 miles. Two expansion programs in 1972 and 1978 led to the development of new mining activity just east of the plant. The original mining pit located west of the facility was expanded farther west during this time.

In the East Pit at Minntac on July 1, 1977, P&H-built shovel No. 31 prepares to take another bite of raw taconite rock for loading into a side-dump car. In the distance, MP15DC switcher No. 971 can be seen pulling out of the East Pit en route to the crusher with 10 carloads of raw taconite. *Steve Glischinski*

At its peak in 1979, the Minntac Railroad had over 40 locomotives—various EMD switchers and Alco RS-3s. Thirty-three ore trains were operated each shift, totaling nearly 200 trips to the mine in each 24-hour period. More than 100 miles of track were in service, some of it double- and four-track mainlines leading to an eight-track crushing plant. Nearly 20 miles of mainline were governed by CTC signaling. Rail and truck mining operations were orchestrated by a pair of dispatchers using a computerized operating system housed in a small building, one of the last towers operated in Minnesota, named "mine control." When the demand for pellets was strong, Minntac's railroad moved just over 50 million tons of crude ore per year. Traffic was so dense on this system that the traditional General Railway Signal relay system for CTC had to be replaced with a computer in 1976 to speed up the response of the CTC system.

Once blasted, crude ore was scooped up by power shovels and loaded directly into side-dump cars or into dump trucks that delivered the ore a short distance to a railcar-loading pocket. A single locomotive pulled trains of up to ten 85-ton-capacity side-dump cars. EMD SW1500 and MP15DC types were purchased in the 1970s to replace older Alcos and Baldwins. The older engines had been brought in from other Oliver Iron Mining/Minnesota Ore Operations installations that were scaled back as natural ore mining was phased out.

USS began experimenting with remote-control on mine locomotives in 1963. Eventually, all Minntac locomotives were so equipped. A single person ran trains in a push-pull fashion, with a locomotive on one end and a cab-equipped side-dump car on the other. Once loaded, trains traveled an average of 5 miles to the crusher, where the operator dismounted, weighed, and dumped each car, all by small, waist-worn remote-control boxes, with which operators could perform virtually all of the same functions they could from the locomotive cab. Later, some rebuilders that bought these locomotives found that the cab controls had frozen from lack of use—operators had used the remotes even from the cabs.

Rail haulage of crude ore met most of Minntac's needs, but rail haulage became less attractive as improvements in truck technology allowed them to carry up to 300 tons of ore and conquer grades of up to 10 percent. Rail operations were sensitive to derailments at key crossovers, and blowing snow in the many temporary pit switches constantly tied up winter operations. Meanwhile, rail haulage costs increased as additional tracks were added, including switchbacks and circle tracks to maintain a steady 1.5 percent grade, and wages increased for the hundreds of people employed in the track gangs that constantly moved pit track to follow the mining shovels and clear areas being blasted. After moving over a billion tons of crude ore by rail in Minntac's first 20 years of operation, studies were conducted on converting to trucks exclusively.

In 1995 officials calculated that in certain applications mine trucks would yield 20 percent cost savings over rail, and trucks began to replace trains in the east end of the West Pit in December 1996. The average truck haul from the east end of the West Pit was 1 1/2 to 2 miles, in contrast to 6 miles by rail. The successful truck application led to the complete conversion of the East Pit to truck haulage in November 1997.

After the East Pit went to trucks, the only rail haul that remained was from the far extremes of the West Pit. The number of locomotives operated in mid-1997 dropped from 20 to 11. Conversion of remaining rail operations to trucks began in 1999, and on November 29 of that year the last train operated from the West Pit to the crusher. Minntac's remaining locomotives were sold off, the locomotive shop at Virginia where heavy repairs were done was closed, and the locomotive shop at Minntac was converted to other uses. Today, the Missabe/CN handles commercial switching on the property.

Minntac switcher No. 959 has just emptied its train of side-dump cars at the crusher and is heading back to the East Pit for a reload. The last East Pit train operated on December 1, 1997. *Steve Glischinski*

An artist's rendering of U.S. Steel's Minntac pellet plant. *Basgen Photography, author collection*

initial annual capacity rated at 6 million tons. At first, production from the original Pilotac plant was incorporated into the new Minntac plant. Pilotac operated as "Line 13," supplementing Minntac concentrate production until 1980. It was torn down in 1990.

Inland Steel's Minorca Mine and Pellet Plant

In 1974 Inland Steel Company, then one of the six largest domestic steel makers, began development of a new taconite-processing facility, the Minorca Mine and Pellet Plant, situated just north of Virginia. The mining of adjacent ore reserves allowed for the crude ore to be trucked directly to the 2.5-million-ton-per-year pellet plant's primary crushers. Its first shipment was on June 9, 1977, and Minorca became the principal source of iron ore for Chicago-based Inland Steel's Indiana Harbor Works at East Chicago, Indiana. Inland specialized in the flat-rolled steel used in automobile bodies and appliances, and in plate steel used for construction applications.

When the Minorca plant was built it was located near the end of DM&IR's old Sliver Branch that at one time served several natural ore mines on the north side of Virginia. However, the Sliver Branch was plagued with numerous street-grade crossings, and with the natural ore mines long since gone, the line was not in good enough shape to handle unit taconite trains. To solve the problem of rail access, DM&IR called upon the Duluth, Winnipeg & Pacific Railway, a subsidiary of the Canadian National Railway. Just south of Virginia, the DM&IR's Virginia Branch crossed the DW&P mainline via a diamond crossing known as Shelton Junction. The Missabe Road obtained trackage rights over DW&P rails northward from Shelton Junction for 6 miles to a new switch, named Minorca Junction, where a short spur provided access to a loop loading track at the Minorca plant. In 1976, the DW&P installed CTC signaling at DM&IR's expense over this stretch of track to better accommodate the Missabe Road's ore trains.

The warmth of spring comes late to Minnesota's "Arrowhead Country." It will be almost June before the grass is green and the trees are leafed out here at Mountain Iron. Just minutes into its journey to Two Harbors, this trainload of steaming pellets departs U.S. Steel's enormous Minntac pellet plant, of which a minor portion looms in the distance. *John Leopard*

An empty train destined for loading at the Minorca pellet plant negotiates the CTC power switch at Minorca Junction on April 4, 1987. Three yellow C&NW covered hopper cars loaded with bentonite clay can be seen on the head end of the train. These cars will be set out at the plant where the contents will be used in the pellet-making process. *Robert C. Anderson*

In the gathering twilight of May 26, 1986, SD9 No. 159 leads a loaded pellet train through the Collingwood interlocking. Smoke from hot brake shoes is visible as the brakes struggle to retard the train's progress downgrade to the Duluth ore docks. *Robert C. Anderson*

CHAPTER FOUR

TRADITION'S END

In the wake of the passage of the Taconite Amendment, eight processing plants were constructed on the Mesabi Range: the three Duluth, Missabe & Iron Range–served plants located in the center of the Range; the Erie and Reserve Mining facilities on the Range's eastern extremity; and a trio of plants served by the Great Northern and later Burlington Northern and Burlington Northern Santa Fe: Butler Taconite near Nashwauk (opened in 1967 and closed in 1985), National Steel Pellet Company at Keewatin (opened in 1967), and

Hibbing Taconite (opened in 1976). As 1970 rolled around the Mesabi Range was down to 32 washing/screening plants processing what was left of the natural ores.

The switch to pellets brought about radical changes in operations and facilities for the Missabe Road. The complexity of mining and shipping natural ore was directly linked to the inconsistency of the ore itself. Because of differing chemical and physical characteristics of natural ore, more than 100 different grades could be found. Even different areas of the same mine shipped different compositions of ore, and each carload of ore could have a specific chemical composition. Steel companies ordered various grades of ore based on what type of steel was to be produced in the blast furnace. In addition, to meet further blending requirements of various steel firms, ore cars were commonly interchanged among the DM&IR and Great Northern, Northern Pacific, and Soo Line at the Twin Ports.

The job of blending the ore as directed by the mining companies fell upon the DM&IR. Each car had to be carefully tracked. Samples taken from groups of cars prior to being picked up at the mines were analyzed so mining companies could predict which cuts of cars should be mixed together to reach the desired blend. Extensive switching at Proctor and Two Harbors was required so that each steel company received the ore it wanted. The actual mixing of the ores was achieved by dumping the desired cuts of cars into predetermined ore-dock pockets, and from there into each boatload.

A train of natural ore mined at the Auburn Mine near Virginia rumbles through downtown Duluth on the Lake Division mainline on October 20, 1994. Once the Auburn Mine ceased shipping natural ore in 2002, natural ore shipments ended for the Missabe Road. Isolated pockets of natural ore remain on the Mesabi Range and may be developed when market conditions dictate. ***Mike Cleary***

In 1960 a pair of new SD9s position a loaded train on top of Dock No. 5 for dumping. Each of Missabe's ore docks, both at Duluth and Two Harbors, had four tracks atop it: a pair of tracks for dumping ore into the pockets of each side of the dock. The dock pockets were built on 12-foot centers, allowing the car doors to be positioned evenly over every other pocket for unloading. Depending on the dock, each pocket could hold four or five carloads of ore. *Basgen Photography, author collection*

Operations of unit taconite trains were much simpler than natural ore trains. Due to the uniform chemical composition of each plant's pellets, switching of the inbound loads was eliminated at the ore-sorting yards in Proctor and Two Harbors.

Another complicating factor in the handling of natural ore was due to its high moisture content—up to 10 percent water—which caused it to freeze in the cars once temperatures dropped below 32 degrees Fahrenheit. During late fall and early spring, ore cars had to be thawed at Proctor and Two Harbors to facilitate dumping on the docks. To soften the ore, steam locomotives were hooked up to a system of

Workers thaw ore cars at Proctor in 1956. A problem with shipping natural ore during the colder months of early spring and late fall was the freezing of the moisture-laden ore in the cars before they could be dumped into the dock pockets. To solve this problem, steam locomotives were coupled to a series of underground steam pipes that were parallel to certain yard tracks at Proctor and Two Harbors. From these underground pipes, workers inserted branch pipes into small holes in the sides of the cars to thaw the ore. ***Basgen Photography, David C. Schauer collection***

pipes that ran along certain yard tracks. These pipes transported steam along the cuts of ore cars, and workers would open small holes in the sides of each car and insert flexible steam hoses and pipes. Once thawed, the cars were quickly forwarded to the docks for dumping. Steam locomotives were also utilized for "slushing" out the ore that became frozen in the dock pockets. Slushing was accomplished by attaching hoses to a steam locomotive and spraying hot water and steam into the pockets, washing the ore down the loading chutes into the ship's cargo hold. Along with the steam locomotives, these large-scale operations required vast amounts of manpower.

After the demise of the steam locomotive, slushing operations in the dock pockets continued with the use of two locomotive tenders that were converted to boiler cars in 1961. Ore-thawing in cars was accomplished using gas-fired infrared installations. The DM&IR pioneered the use of infrared heating for ore-thawing operations. Initial studies began in spring of 1957 and a three-car pilot plant was built at Two Harbors in the fall of that year. Continued studies and tests established the feasibility of using infrared thawing without damaging the ore cars and led to the construction of a 36-car thawing shed (the first of its kind) that was placed in service in 1960.

Due to the more rapid rate of infrared thawing, the installation's capacity was equal to that of the former steaming systems. A similar pocket-mounted system was developed

Steam locomotives 515 and 709 are hooked up to the steam lines at Proctor in 1960. *Lake Superior Railroad Museum, David C. Schauer collection*

This unique view of ore steaming was taken at the south end of Proctor Yard on November 14, 1959. Ore steaming operations with steam locomotives gave way to gas-fired infrared thawing systems: a 36-car thawing shed at Two Harbors and a pocket-mounted version installed on Dock No. 5 in Duluth. The switch to taconite pellets virtually eliminated the freezing problems associated with shipping natural ore. *Robert C. Anderson*

and installed during the fall of 1964 on Dock No. 5 at Duluth. Introduction of the taconite pellet, however, virtually eliminated the freezing problem and the infrared systems were removed from service in Duluth in the early 1970s and from Two Harbors in 1979.

Dock Changes

One effect of winter that taconite pellets could not elude was the annual freezing of the Great Lakes, resulting in the halt of all shipping. But the immense cost of the pellet plants required them to run 365 days a year. To accommodate pellets produced during the winter, the Missabe completed its Lakehead Taconite Storage Facility near Dock No. 6 in Duluth in 1965. Built with an initial capacity of 2.5 million tons, this facility was later expanded to 3 million tons of on-ground storage space. A 40-acre site of reclaimed land on the east side of

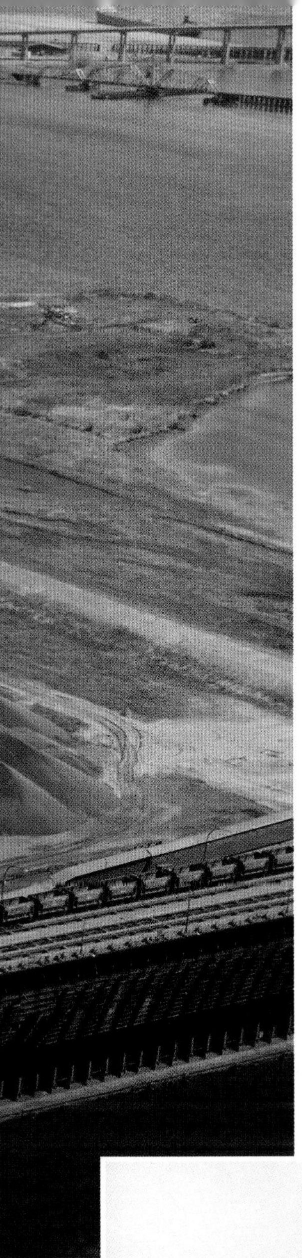

Duluth's Dock No. 6 and the adjacent Lakehead Taconite Storage Facility as seen from the air in 1977. Separate piles are maintained for each company's pellet output. *Basgen Photography, Dan Mackey collection*

Dock No. 6 was filled in with dredged sand and other materials to accommodate the storage piles. The original Duluth, Missabe & Northern coal dock was dismantled to make way for the new pellet storage area.

To feed the stockpile, the inner 64 pockets on the east side of Dock No. 6 were modified to allow them to dump onto a 36-inch-wide conveyor that transports pellets to and from the storage area. A traveling, rail-mounted stacker piles the pellets. When the shipping season begins each spring, a self-propelled bucket-wheel reclaimer scoops up the stockpiled pellets. This machine places pellets back onto the conveyor for a return trip to Dock No. 6's loading pockets.

As more plants were opened and others increased production, DM&IR was forced to keep up with the shipping demands. Another factor entered into the mix in 1972 when huge 1,000-foot-long ore carriers began plying the Great Lakes. The first of them, Bethlehem Steel Corporation's *Stewart J. Cort*, loaded its first cargo, 49,343 tons of pellets, at Two Harbors on May 5, 1972. At more than three

The stackers at both Duluth and Two Harbors travel on railroad tracks atop an elevated berm and can build piles on either side of the berm to a height of 75 feet. The stockpiling rate for these machines is 6,000 tons per hour. *Basgen Photography, author collection*

Wheel flanges squeal as a loaded Minorca train negotiates the connecting track between the DW&P and DM&IR at Shelton Junction in the fall of 1987. The track continuing across the diamond crossing is DM&IR's Virginia Branch. The headlight in the distance is a T-Bird crude-ore train that has just finished loading at the Thunderbird north loadout. ***Otto P. Dobnick***

football fields in length, the *Cort* was followed by a dozen more 1,000-footers in the next decade, each capable of loading up to 60,000 tons of pellets. Of these, U.S. Steel operated three: the *Presque Isle* tug-barge, leased by U.S. Steel starting in 1973; the *Edwin H. Gott*, constructed in 1979; and the *Edgar B. Speer*, built in 1980. U.S. Steel also launched the *Roger Blough* in 1972, a boat midway between the traditional ore boats and the 1,000-footers, at 105 feet wide and 848 feet long.

With the expansions of Minntac in 1972 and 1976 and Eveleth Taconite in 1976, and the construction of Minorca in 1976, DM&IR outgrew the pellet-storage facility in Duluth. There were experimental attempts by U.S. Steel to run the ore boats year-round, but Lake Superior eventually won out and the boats went back to seasonal operation. The winter-storage capacity at the docks had to be expanded.

Thanks to its better winter ice conditions, a shorter trip by water to the Soo, and more available land, Two Harbors received wholesale changes, beginning in 1976. Beginning in August of that year, the entire ore-sorting yard was removed to make room for a 2-million-ton-capacity stockpile area. The facility was dedicated on September 13, 1978, and on-ground storage capacity was expanded in late 1979 to hold an additional 500,000 tons. The Two Harbors system differs from the Duluth installation in that incoming trains are either dumped in motion at an onshore dump house or on the dock. The pellets can likewise be conveyed to a stockpile area.

However, the 1,000-footers were too wide to be loaded evenly by the existing docks in Two Harbors. To overcome this, initially the boats were loaded from one side and then either pulled across to an adjacent dock or turned in the harbor and loaded on the other side; a better way had to be found.

A key feature of the Two Harbors conversion was a new ship-loading system tailored to the wider 1,000-foot vessels. The west side of

Reclaim from stockpile is achieved by a crawler-mounted bucketwheel reclaimer that scoops the pellets and places them back onto the reversible conveyor system for a return trip to the top of the dock. These machines are capable of reclaiming 1,500 tons of pellets per hour. *Basgen Photography, author collection*

On September 1, 1997, Great Lakes Fleet self-unloading vessel *Roger Blough* sits low in Agate Bay after taking on a load of taconite pellets at Two Harbors' Dock No. 2. The 858-foot-long vessel was named for the retired chairman of U.S. Steel's board of directors. The numbered conveyor belt-equipped shuttle conveyors can be seen in both the upright and horizontal loading position just above the ship. *David C. Schauer*

Dock No. 2 was modified by removing the old loading chutes, pocket doors, and operating equipment. In their place were 22 conveyor belt–equipped shuttle conveyors, each capable of extending over the vessels' hatches. This design extended the reach of the dock, providing more uniform loading of the wider vessels.

As more 1,000-foot ore carriers came into service, it soon became apparent that the outmoded Duluth dock facilities would also require a ship-loader system. Lessons learned with the completion of the Two Harbors ship-loader were incorporated into the design of the upgraded Duluth system. Dock No. 6 went through a three-year, $26 million modernization project that saw the addition of 20 ship-loading conveyors similar to the ones at Two Harbors. In addition, a new office and service center for dock operations was constructed adjacent to Dock No. 6. The first vessel to load from the new Duluth ship-loader was the *Columbia Star*, operated by Oglebay Norton, on July 19, 1983.

Ore Car Modifications

While pellets are just as dense as natural ore, a standard carload of pellets is lighter than a carload of natural ore because of the air space between the pellets. As a result, hundreds of DM&IR ore cars were modified with top-mounted side extensions to increase their cubic capacity. The first cars modified for pellet and crude-ore service were 70-ton-capacity cars that had 19 1/2-inch extensions added in 1965. To signify their specialized status, these cars were renumbered by changing the first digit of each to a 5. To prevent the modified cars from being overloaded at the mines, the side-extension height was lowered in 1971 to 9 3/4 inches, resulting in this series of cars being labeled as "mini." To distinguish them, pellet cars equipped with side extensions are generally referred to as "high-sides," while unmodified ore cars are known as "regulars" or "low-sides."

Winter operation also posed the problem of air leakage from train brake lines at hose couplings. This resulted in the need to operate more frequent and shorter trains. To avoid reductions in train size during winter operations, the Missabe permanently coupled groups of four ore cars with drawbars, eliminating not only the angle cocks and hose connections, but three sets of couplers and most of the slack action, plus much of the maintenance expense. Permanently coupling the cars together could be justified because switching of the ore cars was virtually eliminated by the unit-train operations afforded by taconite pellets. The first of these sets, dubbed "mini-quads," were assembled in 1972. To more easily identify the coupler-equipped ends of each quad set, the end posts of that car were painted bright orange.

With the introduction of the mini-quads there also came a new air-brake system for Missabe ore trains. The Missabe's ore trains descend a maximum 3 percent grade into Two Harbors and a grade reaching 2.2 percent down Proctor Hill into Duluth. Safe operation down the two hills requires the use of retainers, which involves presetting some air pressure on each car's trainline brakes by turning a handle on the side of the car. This task was performed manually by the brakeman walking the length of the train. The time consumed setting up the retainers at the top of the hill and knocking them down at the bottom meant that certain runs could not be consistently completed within the federally mandated 12-hour on-duty time limit for crews.

The new braking system was adopted from one developed by Westinghouse Air Brake Company for U.S. Steel's Orinoco Mine railroad in Venezuela, which had similar problems with steep grades and heavy trains. The "Orinoco Retainer Control" is a separate airline operated by the engineer and used to hold and, when necessary, to modulate an initial automatic brake-pipe reduction. With the Orinoco system in use, the automatic brake pipe could be recharged to full pressure without releasing the initial application, in effect setting a train's worth of retainers from the cab while moving at speed, all with the twist of a single handle. This eliminated the need to stop the train while the brakeman set the retainer pressure on each car.

Automatic Car Identification

Pioneering technology came to the Missabe Road in fall of 1964 with test operations of an optical car-tracking system. Developed by the Sylvania Electronic Division of the General Telephone and Electronics Corporation (GTE) in collaboration with the Association of American Railroads (AAR), the system was designed to keep track of the more than two million freight cars then in service in the United States and Canada.

Named Kartrak, or as it became more popularly known, ACI (Automatic Car Identification), the system consists of three major components: a label, a scanner, and a decoder. A color-coded label mounted on the side of each car consists of 13 small horizontal stripes in single colors or combinations of blue, black, red, and white. These stripes, when arranged in proper sequence, are used to identify the car's reporting marks, number, and light weight. The reflective labels were developed by Minnesota-based 3M Company and made out of a material similar to that used in making road signs. Trackside scanning devices, developed by Sylvania, shine a beam of white light onto the ACI labels while the cars pass by at speeds of up to 80 miles per hour. The

In 1956 the ACI reader at the north end of Proctor Yard scans the colored labels of an inbound loaded ore train. As the cars were weighed, ACI information, such as the car's weight and contents, was sent to a computer where it was deciphered and then forwarded by teletype to yard and dock offices, the Iron Junction Operations Center, and the mining companies. *Basgen Photography, author collection*

scanner is an electro-optical device that converts the color-coded data of each label into electronic analog signals that are sent to the decoder's computers for deciphering.

Installation of the scanners began on the DM&IR in August 1964 at the south end of Proctor Yard, followed by units installed at the ore scales at the north end of the yard a month later. These early components of the system became operational in the middle of October 1964. Scanners were eventually deployed at the scales at Highland and Allen Junction, both on the Two Harbors Line, and at Alborn, on the Missabe Division.

Kartrak/ACI was adopted by the AAR, which required all rolling stock operated in interchange service nationwide to have labels applied beginning in 1967. Problems with maintaining the immense number of labels made the system very expensive to operate, however. Scratches and dirt accumulation on the labels often resulted in scanners misreading the information. The system's accuracy was much less than expected and it was officially dropped by the AAR in 1978. However, the DM&IR continued to use ACI. This was due to a car fleet that is mainly captive to home rails, thus allowing better maintenance of the labels, which are kept clean by an automatic washer, located at the north end of Proctor Yard, that rinses the labels as they pass. The ACI system was a precursor to today's highly successful Automatic Equipment Identification (AEI) that uses a more reliable radio/magnetic transponder technology impervious to dirt.

Later Track Abandonment

In 1973 shipments of natural ore were eclipsed by taconite loadings for the first time on the Missabe Road. As more and more natural ore mines closed, mine spurs and branchline trackage followed into oblivion. Notable abandonments included nearly 15 miles of the Eastern Mesaba Branch in 1961, the majority of the Hull-Rust Short Line in 1962, a portion of the Superior Branch from Wolf to Sherwood in 1967, and 7 miles of the Wales Branch between Forest Center and Sawbill Junction in 1977. In 1982 a major portion of the original Duluth & Iron Range mainline through Ely, 35 miles of track between Winton and Embarrass, was abandoned. The following year, another 24-mile chunk of the Wales Branch came up between Sawbill Junction and Jordan.

As mining operations waned, there came operational changes on the western end of the system. In 1974 the Missabe Road began operating most of its ore trains destined for the remaining Canisteo District mines via trackage rights over the Burlington Northern between Emmert and Holman Junction. This rendered the Alborn Branch obsolete and it was later abandoned in its entirety in 1977. Missabe's final west-end ore customer was U.S. Steel's Arcturus Mine, which ceased operations in October 1981. Missabe continued to handle some natural ore from the Canisteo plant, originating on the BN and interchanged at Wilpen, until 1984. By this time BN's natural ore docks in Allouez had been closed and operations there were transferred to their new taconite-loading facility.

Keenan Yard

As the natural ore mines closed, the need for the ore-sorting yards scattered across the Iron

June 29, 2004, finds two 400-series locomotives rumbling past the scale house at Highland. In-motion scales for weighing trains are located at both Highland on the Iron Range Division and at the north end of Proctor Yard for Missabe Division runs. The silver apparatus near the scale house is an ACI reader. *Kevin Madsen*

Most of the original D&IR main to Ely was removed in 1982, but a 6-mile portion was retained to serve the Erie Mining/LTV Steel Mining Company plant at Hoyt Lakes (Hinsdale station on the DM&IR). Another 4.6 miles of track from Hinsdale to Embarrass were also retained for pulpwood loading, but this segment was removed in 1993. On March 7, 1986, a pair of Missabe high-nose SD18s leads a short six-car train of pulpwood through the snow-covered landscape near Hinsdale. *Doug Buell*

Range ceased. The yards at Mitchell, Bovey, Hull-Rust, Soudan, and Hibbing were gradually phased out as neighboring mines closed. As early as 1956, plans were being drawn up for a consolidated ore-marshalling yard near Wolf that would serve as a gathering point for ore mined in the Hibbing, Chisholm, Mountain

Iron, Fraser, and Virginia-Fayal districts. The business slump of the early 1960s shelved this plan and it would be nearly 10 years before they actually came to fruition. When the taconite business improved, again there was a need for a new yard at the north end of the system.

Ground was broken for the Keenan Yard in spring 1976, but it was not to be located at Wolf, as originally called for in the plans of the late 1950s. The new yard was located just off the Proctor–to–Mountain Iron mainline at the junction with the Shaw Cut-off. Keenan's central location allowed it to meet the needs of the Minntac, Eveleth, and Minorca pellet plants, as well as various freight customers in the Virginia area. Built on filled-in swamp, the yard includes 16 tracks, a locomotive servicing area, car repair, and maintenance-of-way facilities. Keenan was opened for operations in October 1976, and on March 29, 1985, all north-end transportation department personnel and train-dispatching were moved there from Iron Junction, which had been the operation headquarters since the days of the Merritts and their DM&N.

After Keenan Yard's opening, operations at Biwabik and Rainy Junction were greatly reduced. Rainy Junction Yard, located just southwest of Virginia, had once been the hub of DM&IR's operations on the central portion of the Range. It was home terminal for many mine-run and commercial-freight crews. Nearby was Oliver Mining Company's

With natural ore loads from the High Grade Yard near Bovey, SD9 No. 116 leads sister 174 and SD18 No. 190 eastbound past the depot at Nashwauk on Burlington Northern tracks on May 25, 1978. The new Highway 169 overpass looms above the train. While there are extensive reserves of natural ore left in the area, DM&IR's ore train operations on the western Mesabi Range were largely finished by 1981. *Robert C. Anderson*

Biwabik was once a focal point for ore operations served by both of the Missabe Road's predecessor companies, each of which had yards and branches to serve nearby mining operations. In this late 1960s view at Biwabik, motive power for two mine runs congregates near the yard office while the train of empty cars that the photographer is riding arrives from Proctor. This yard office was built in the late 1950s; a similar structure was constructed at Rainy Junction in 1960. *Patrick C. Dorin*

Rouchleau ore-crushing plant, once a major Missabe customer. Rouchleau's crushing operations were suspended in 1975, and the crusher dismantled in 1986. As a result, the former interchange point with the Duluth, Winnipeg & Pacific was moved a few miles south to Shelton Junction.

Biwabik Yard was reduced to a ghost yard as well. Like Rainy Junction, Biwabik had called many mine runs, assembled their loads into trains, and forwarded them to yards at both Two Harbors and Proctor. At one time, Biwabik was one of the busiest ore-gathering yards on the Mesabi Range and featured a four-stall engine house, modern yard office/tower, and layover facilities for road crews from Two Harbors. After its operational demise, the yard office and many of the yard tracks were removed, while the roundhouse to this day is used as a base for local track maintenance forces.

With natural-ore tonnage in rapid decline, Keenan Yard was built in 1976 to consolidate all yard-switching operations conducted on the north end of the Missabe into one location, replacing yards at Mitchell, Rainy Junction, Fayal, and Biwabik. On June 30, 2004, the Keenan Switch is at the north end of Keenan Yard. The CTC-controlled switches at either end of the yard are named Northgate and Southgate. The BN covered hoppers contain bentonite, a clay used in the pellet-making process. *Kevin Madsen*

On an unspecified date in 1949, Yellowstone No. 236 gets under way at Rainy Junction Yard with a loaded train of ore destined for Proctor. The impressive structure looming in the background is the Rouchleau ore crusher and treatment facility that served a group of mines near Virginia operated by the Oliver Iron Mining Company. Short trains of freshly mined coarse ore were shoved into the top of the structure via the high trestle and dumped into the crusher. *Iron Range Historical Society, Gilbert, Minnesota*

Fall colors come early to the Iron Range as seen in this September 26, 1987, view of a loaded Minntac pellet train at the east end of Biwabik. The empty yard tracks are testimony to the opening of Keenan Yard that consolidated the operations of a number of separate yards. *Robert C. Anderson*

Interstate Branch Transformation

Interstate highway construction is not often associated with increased rail traffic, but that is exactly what happened for the Spirit Lake/Interstate Branch. In 1975 a program was initiated to extend Interstate 35/U.S. Highway 61 through the congested downtown area of Duluth. Standing in the way was the Bridge Yard, co-owned by the Burlington Northern and Chicago & North Western. It was at this yard that BN, C&NW, and the Milwaukee Road interchanged traffic with the Duluth, Winnipeg & Pacific, better known locally as "the Peg." The DW&P route was used to funnel traffic from the U.S./Canadian border to the Twin Ports, where cars could be handed off to connecting carriers for forwarding throughout the Midwest.

The DW&P reached its namesake city in 1912 and crammed its yard facilities into a small area of West Duluth. To reach Duluth,

Left: The DW&P/CN mainline from the north connects with DM&IR's Spirit Lake/Interstate Branch at Nopeming Junction. DW&P/CN trains then operate over DM&IR rails to reach their Pokegama Yard in South Superior. Dropping down the steep 1.98 percent grade at Nopeming Junction on a colorful October 9, 1994, is a loaded taconite train destined for Geneva Steel in Utah. The Geneva Steel contract was one of the busier all-rail movements, handling over a million tons per year, until Geneva shut down its mill in November 2001. *John Leopard*

Below: At Saunders, just south of Superior, Wisconsin, the GN/BN/BNSF main route into the Twin Ports crossed over the Interstate Branch at a 90-degree angle. Over time, connecting tracks were built in three of the crossing's quadrants, allowing other railroads easy access to the Missabe's line. The C&NW, and later UP, was a tenant of Missabe's Interstate Branch between Saunders and South Itasca. In October 1985, a C&NW train from Minneapolis, en route to South Itasca, uses the connecting track known as the "BN Connection," while the DM&IR Steelton Switch crew waits. The white building in the distance is Saunders Tower, which was razed by BN and replaced with a small shack to house a small control machine for the interlocking plant. *Otto P. Dobnick*

the Peg traversed a steep 1.15 percent grade carved into the face of the glacial hills surrounding Duluth, the same obstacles encountered on the DM&IR Proctor Hill route and the Spirit Lake Branch. In addition, to reach Bridge Yard the Peg utilized a maintenance-intensive route that traversed a massive timber trestle. The DW&P was a more-than-willing partner in the relocation of their Duluth operations. It was agreed that Bridge Yard would be vacated by November 1984.

The costs associated with the move would be borne by both the Federal Highway Administration and the Minnesota Department of Transportation. Understandably, Minnesota state officials preferred to keep the high-paying DW&P jobs and resulting tax base in the Gopher State. They supported a plan to revamp and expand DM&IR's Steelton Yard, which sat little used since the closing of U.S. Steel's Duluth Works. But residents of the area objected to the plan and a new site was

On March 6, 1991, DW&P SD40 No. 5911 is assisted by two similar CN models as they grind up Steelton Hill with train No. 401 at a location known as Short Line Park. The DW&P had ten SD40 units on its roster that were originally built for sister CN subsidiary railroad Grand Trunk Western. Once attaining home rails at Nopeming Junction, No. 401 will travel 160 miles to reach the Canadian border at Ranier, Minnesota, just east of International Falls. ***John Leopard***

selected in Wisconsin, just south of Superior. It was still to be located along the DM&IR Interstate Branch, at the former DM&IR/Northern Pacific junction known as Pokegama, named for a nearby river. The NP track had been abandoned by the BN in 1975.

Construction of the 210-acre facility began in July 1983. Because the new yard was built on swampland, over 400,000 cubic yards of fill were hauled in, spread, and compacted. Twelve miles of track, all of it continuous-welded rail, were then laid on top of the fill, and a new 13,000-square-foot administrative building was completed, along with a new three-track locomotive and car repair shop.

To reach its new yard, the DW&P secured trackage rights over DM&IR's Interstate Branch. A new connection was cut in near Nopeming, where the Peg mainline crossed over the Missabe on a timber trestle. To handle the increase in train traffic, Missabe upgraded the two branches during 1984, as the little-used line with its 112-pound jointed rail and lack of signaling was hardly up to the task. Missabe installed new ties, ballast, and 132-pound continuous-welded rail, as well as CTC signaling operated by the Missabe South dispatcher in Keenan. Soon after the new yard opened on November 1, 1984, the Peg abandoned their line down Spirit Mountain and the West Duluth yard facilities were removed.

The Interstate Branch had other tenants, including heavy use by Canadian National. In 1981, for example, the C&NW began operating over the Interstate Branch between Saunders and its main Twin Ports yard at Itasca, located in far eastern Superior. This allowed the C&NW to abandon the southerly portion of their Minneapolis–to–Spooner, Wisconsin, line, a former Omaha Road route, in favor of trackage rights over BN between Minneapolis and Saunders. Union Pacific inherited these trackage rights with its purchase of the C&NW in 1995.

Wisconsin Central, likewise, became a heavy user of the Interstate Branch, dating to the company's formation in 1987. These rights allowed the WC to interchange with the DW&P at Pokegama Yard and with the BN (and later BNSF) at 28th Street Yard in Superior. Wishing a line of its own to Chicago, CN purchased the WC in October 2001. The 17-mile gap in CN ownership between Nopeming Junction and South Itasca soon became a thorn in CN's operating plan, however, and the Interstate Branch's strategic importance to the Canadian National would be a key reason for CN's purchase of the DM&IR.

Large, well-built steel bridges were a hallmark of the Missabe Road. A number of them were located along the Spirit Lake/Interstate Branch, including this one at the south end of Steelton Yard. On a cold January 22, 1996, an empty all-rail train off the Wisconsin Central is about to arrive in the yard. This particular train operated between U.S. Steel's Gary Works in Indiana and Minntac using tracks of the EJ&E, WC, and, of course, the DM&IR. ***John Leopard***

In double-track territory, the DM&IR favors "left-handed" operation, opposite of how we drive cars in the United States. In August 1991, a Geneva all-rail train (note the coal hoppers) is about to pass under Highway 37 at Keenan. Since the taconite pellets are much more dense than coal, only about half of a standard coal hopper can be loaded. *John Leopard*

CHAPTER FIVE

MISSABE IN MODERN TIMES

In the late 1970s the nation's steel industry was in as good a shape as it had ever been, with a pair of new taconite plants opened on the Range. Bethlehem Steel Corporation's Hibbing Taconite plant, served by Burlington Northern, went into operation in 1976, producing just over 6 million tons annually. A year later, in 1977, Inland Steel's Minorca operation began production. Other existing plants added production capacity.

At the passing siding at Coons, a meet is executed between a Minntac-loaded pellet train led by SD38-2 No. 209 and a loaded Minntac-bound limestone train with SD-M No. 314 in charge. Coons is one of three passing sidings on the Missabe Division mainline between Proctor and Keenan (the others are at Alborn and Kelsey). Each passing siding, created when the second main track was removed between Fairlane and Carson in 1988, was equipped with a dispatcher-controlled power switch at the south end and a spring switch at the north end. *John Leopard*

Minntac underwent an expansion in 1972 and another in 1978 that more than doubled its original tonnage output to 18.5 million, making it the largest taconite plant in North America. In 1974, ownership of the Fairlane plant changed hands and the operation was renamed Eveleth Mines. Fairlane was expanded in 1976 to produce 6 million tons annually. At the same time, a second mining pit, Thunderbird South, was developed.

But as the 1980s dawned, the health of the domestic integrated steel makers proved to be anything but good. Most of the blast furnaces and rolling mills had been producing steel since the turn of the century with little investment made to modernize these facilities. This resulted in a domestic industry that was unable to compete against less expensive imports, and by 1980 foreign steel made up nearly one-quarter of the steel consumed in the United States. American mills accounted for 20 percent of the world's total steel production in 1970; by 1984 this share had plummeted to 12 percent.

The last of a string of good years for integrated steel makers and pellet producers came in 1979. Late that year, U.S. Steel announced the closure of many of its outdated facilities.

By the time this June 9, 1992, photo was taken at the west end of Biwabik, many of the yard tracks had been removed. This train of empty mini-quad cars is destined for loading at Minntac. *John Leopard*

Others, such as Armco, Bethlehem, Jones & Laughlin, and Youngstown Sheet & Tube, soon followed suit. In an effort to stay financially healthy, U.S. Steel began to diversify by investing outside the industry. In spring 1982, U.S. Steel acquired the Marathon Oil Company and then expanded its energy holdings when it purchased Texas Oil & Gas Corporation in 1986. To better reflect its new image, the steel giant changed its name to USX Corporation in 1986. The Minntac plant, after producing over 16 million tons of pellets in 1979, made only 3.4 million tons three years later, in 1982.

Other steel makers also felt the pressure. Ford Motor Company spun off its steel-making unit to Rouge Steel. In April 1985, Wheeling-Pittsburgh Steel Company, the nation's seventh-largest steel producer, filed for bankruptcy, resulting in the closure of Butler Taconite. A year later, LTV Steel Corporation was in the same precarious position. LTV Steel, operator of the one-time Jones & Laughlin Steel, Republic Steel, and Youngstown Sheet & Tube properties, was formed in 1984 and was the partial owner of both the Reserve and Erie mining properties. LTV's bankruptcy, and Armco's reluctance to support Reserve on their own, led to the sudden shutdown of Reserve in 1986 in favor of operating the Erie plant at full capacity. Ownership of Erie was consolidated by LTV and the facility renamed LTV Steel Mining Company. The Reserve

Clouds of brake-shoe smoke are a common sight as engineers attempt to retard their trains' progress while descending steep grades into the Lake Superior Basin at Duluth, Steelton, and Two Harbors. The low sun of a late February 6, 2000, afternoon accents the brake-shoe smoke coming off the friction-bearing-trucked C&NW ore cars of a loaded Minorca "E-rail" as it drops into the north end of Steelton Yard. *Kent Rengo*

facilities were later reopened by new owner Cyprus Minerals in 1989 under the name Cyprus Northshore Mining Company.

Taconite pellets made at the Fairlane plant scurry through Coons on the Missabe Division mainline. SD9 No. 162 leads the way on this pleasant October 10, 1989, day. By the time the last steam-powered ore train operated on the Missabe Road on July 5, 1960, the company had acquired a total of 74 SD9s from builder EMD. *John Leopard*

Transtar

Although the steel industry was rebounding, steel made up only 30 percent of USX's revenues in 1988. To emphasize its new focus and to reduce debt incurred in making its oil and gas acquisitions, USX decided to spin off its transportation subsidiaries. Early that year USX formed the subsidiary company Transtar to hold the stock of its transportation properties, which included eight railroads. Then, in June 1988, USX announced that it would part with its majority share of Transtar, selling out to Wall Street investment firm Blackstone Capital Partners for $500 million. USX

Continued on page 110

North Shore Scenic Railroad

After the last run of passenger train No. 6 between Ely and Duluth on July 15, 1961, the 26-mile-long Lake Division led a quiet existence. Normal freight operations called for an Iron Range Division crew to bring a freight train from Two Harbors to Duluth in the late afternoon. At Endion, this crew would meet a counterpart train from Proctor. The crews would exchange trains at Endion and return back to their respective terminals. The main commodities handled by these trains during this period were bentonite and other mining supplies for Reserve and Erie Mining, pulpwood (mainly gathered along the Wales Branch), and plywood siding from the Louisiana-Pacific plant at Two Harbors. These trains were also utilized to ferry locomotives between Two Harbors and the shops at Proctor.

With much of their wood traffic lost to trucks, and looking for a way to trim expenses, the DM&IR ended regular operations over the Lake Division in 1982 in favor of routing freight traffic "around the horn" by way of Iron Junction and Biwabik. The final trains operated by the Missabe Road over the then-out-of-service line were a pair of passenger specials on July 28 and 29, 1984. These trains were used to commemorate the one hundredth anniversary of the first shipment of iron ore from the Vermilion Range. The trips were sponsored by the Lake Superior Museum of Transportation, a rail museum housed in Duluth's Union Depot and now known as the Lake Superior Railroad Museum (LSRM).

After the 1984 passenger excursions, the line again sat unused, but hardly unnoticed. Museum and local government officials saw the potential for a tourist railroad along the line that closely skirted

Passengers prepare to board Northshore Scenic Railroad RDC No. 9169 at Two Harbors on a pleasant August 5, 1990. The Budd RDC was built in 1951 for the Chicago & North Western and the depot was constructed by the D&IR in 1907. On display near the depot are two steam locomotives built by Baldwin: former D&IR 2-6-0 No. 3 and one of the heralded DM&IR Yellowstones, No. 229. ***Steve Glischinski***

the Lake Superior shoreline. One of the chief proponents of saving the line was Donald B. Shank, who in 1981 retired as vice president and general manager of the DM&IR. Shank had been instrumental in establishing the Duluth museum and in getting DM&IR involved in donating equipment. In 1986 the St. Louis and Lake County Regional Rail Authority was formed to purchase the line and in 1988 the authority did just that for $1.5 million. The DM&IR retained trackage rights over the route, although it rarely used them.

Tourist operations did not begin until 1990 due to freeway construction in downtown Duluth, the same project that saw the DW&P yards moved from West Duluth to Pokegama. The Rail Authority purchased a Budd Company–built RDC1 from the Blue Mountain & Reading Railroad for immediate service, with a variety of other equipment from the museum's collection also being utilized that first year, during which 37,000 passengers rode the new railroad.

The Rail Authority contracted various operators for the railroad until 1996, when the LSRM took over operations, utilizing the existing name of North Shore Scenic Railway. With the exception of RDC1 No. 9169, owned by the Rail Authority, the museum provided rolling stock and locomotives that included a former Soo Line FP7 and an ex-GN/BN NW5. On May 18, 1998, DM&IR donated chop-nose SD18 No. 193 to the museum.

Regularly scheduled trains operate on the North Shore Scenic from May to October, with daily operations during the peak Memorial Day–Labor Day tourist season. Trips to Two Harbors include a stop at the former D&IR depot, which houses the Lake County Historical Society Museum. Shorter trips are available, and in addition to regular excursions, the railroad operates special "Pizza Trains" on certain evenings during the summer months.

Visit the Lake Superior Railroad Museum Web site: www.lsrm.org

In May 1998, the DM&IR donated SD18 No. 193 to the Lake Superior Railroad Museum where it is kept busy hauling tourists along the shores of Lake Superior—a job no doubt less demanding than lugging carloads of iron ore. Shown towing a railfan excursion on September 11, 2004, No. 193 crosses over the Knife River near the village of the same name. *Kevin Madsen*

On the point of 55 carloads of fluxstone destined for Minntac is a pair of SD-Ms, spliced by SD9 No. 134. The northward train is about to pass under the DW&P mainline at Munger on September 25, 1990. The roadbed of the abandoned second main track is visible alongside the existing main track. ***John Leopard***

would retain a 44 percent share of Transtar, with senior management of the transportation companies holding a 5 percent share. Blackstone officially took over Transtar on December 28, 1988.

In addition to the DM&IR, Transtar acquired the Bessemer & Lake Erie; Birmingham Southern; Lake Terminal; McKeesport Connecting; Union Railroad; and the Elgin, Joliet & Eastern. Also included were USX's water transportation subsidiaries, Warrior & Gulf Navigation, Pittsburgh & Conneaut Dock, and the U.S. Steel Great Lakes Fleet, one of the biggest bulk carriers on the Great Lakes. Altogether, Transtar employed 4,000 people and oversaw 2,000 miles of track, some 300 locomotives, 20,000 railroad cars, 14 lake vessels, 305 barges, and 27 tugboats.

The DM&IR, and the steel industry in general, emerged from the wreckage of the 1980s much smaller and leaner. Total tonnage for pellets hauled by the Missabe Road stabilized around 20 million tons per year throughout the 1990s. During the 20-year period from 1974 to 1994, domestic steel-producing capacity was halved from 158 million tons to 77 million. However, for the same period, capacity of the nation's electric-arc furnace "minimills" surged from 8 million tons to 37 million. The rise of the nation's minimills—generally defined as mills that melt scrap metal in large electric furnaces to

Self-unloading bulk carrier *Joseph L. Block* is seen pouring fluxstone into the receiving hopper on the west side of Dock No. 6 on July 22, 2001. This 728-foot-long vessel was built for the Inland Steel Company and launched on February 26, 1976, with a capacity of 37,200 tons and the ability to discharge up to 6,000 tons of material per hour through its 250-foot-long boom. The fluxstone will be transported by conveyor belt to Missabe's Bulk Receiving Materials Facility (BRMF) located just east of Dock No. 6, where it will be stockpiled and later loaded into railcars. *David C. Schauer*

promote molten steel—came about in the mid-1980s. Due to less handling of raw materials, a minimill's facilities can be smaller than those of an integrated steel producer, hence the name. By the mid-1990s the minimill moniker was no longer accurate, as some of these plants could now melt, cast, and roll more steel than some integrated mills. Minimills could also produce low-grade steel cheaper than their integrated counterparts as long as the product's surface quality was not a concern. To the detriment of the taconite producers, the minimills' principal raw material was scrap metal, not taconite pellets.

Fluxstone

The Missabe Road got a shot in the arm when taconite-processing plants began producing a new type of pellet, called a fluxed pellet. In traditional steel-making, a limestone/dolomite blend was added directly into the blast furnace. But in the late 1980s the industry found that adding the limestone mixture at the pellet plant was not only cheaper for the steel mill, but also produced a higher-quality pellet. The limestone mixture, also called fluxstone, combines chemically with unwanted impurities in the iron ore and coke and carries them out of the blast furnace in a liquid form called slag. Fluxstone consists of a roughly 50/50

The press release accompanying this photo stated, "Oscar Rinell, General Foreman of Jones & Laughlin's Schley Mine Group, places the traditional cleanup broom in the last carload of iron ore to be shipped from the Schley pits." This tradition signified a "clean sweep" and was used to signal the end of a mine's production. J&L closed down the Schley pits near Gilbert in September 1969 after producing more than 37 million tons of ore over a period of 60 years. *Iron Range Historical Society, Gilbert, Minnesota*

blend of limestone (calcium carbonate) and dolomite (calcium and magnesium carbonate), both quarried in Michigan's upper and lower peninsulas. Pellets that do not contain limestone are called standard or acid pellets.

Minntac began testing the manufacture of fluxed pellets in the fall of 1985, and by 1988 a large share of the plant's pellet output was of the fluxed variety. Inland Steel's Minorca Plant introduced a fluxed pellet at roughly the same time as Minntac and eventually converted their entire 2.5-million-ton output to fluxed pellets. The Eveleth plant has never produced a fluxed pellet per se, but does add a small amount of crushed limestone to its pellets, which arrived in covered hoppers via the Duluth, Winnipeg & Pacific.

Fluxstone soon became second only to pellets in tonnage hauled by the Missabe. The stone comes from three Michigan ports, Calcite (limestone), Cedarville (dolomite), and Port Inland (both). Both types are delivered by lake boat to Duluth and then transported by conveyor belt to storage piles east of Dock No. 6. Initially, the rock was unloaded at Hallett Dock Company's Dock No. 5, immediately adjacent to the ore docks, and was transferred into DM&IR ore cars using front-end loaders. Hallett Dock was served by Burlington Northern, which pulled and spotted the loading tracks, with the exchange of cars between the two roads taking place at nearby Missabe Junction.

Hallett Dock handled inbound limestone for both Minntac and Minorca until July 1995, when Minntac contacted the Missabe about handling its fluxstone directly, bypassing handling and switching charges incurred from Hallett and BN. Missabe built an unloading hopper on the west side of Dock No. 6 to receive the limestone, using an existing conveyor that normally emptied the dock pockets to transfer the limestone to the storage facility. With a new commodity handled through the dock, the name of the storage facility was changed from Lakehead Storage Facility to the Bulk Materials Receiving Facility (BMRF). Hallett continued to handle fluxstone for Minorca until 2001 when the DM&IR won that business. Minntac generally receives just over a million tons of fluxstone annually, with Minorca taking around 300,000 tons each year.

No More Natural Ore

Minnesota's iron ore industry saw a banner year in 1995 as the nation's steel makers continued to enjoy a high demand for steel. At more than 51 million tons, 1995 marked the fourth consecutive year of growth in domestic steel output. The DM&IR reaped the benefits of this success. Minntac turned out 13.6 million tons of flux pellets, and Eveleth Mines saw near-capacity production at its facility with 5.2 million tons. Inland Steel's Minorca plant was not left out, producing a record 2.75 million tons of pellets. On December 1, 1996, the ownership of Eveleth Mines changed again, and the company became known as EVTAC Mining, with ownership split among Rouge Steel, AK Steel, and Stelco.

When operations ceased at the Donora and Stephens mines on the eastern Range on September 6, 1991, it was believed to mark the first time in over 100 years that no natural ore would be extracted from the ground of northern Minnesota. The Stephens property was first mined by Oliver Iron Mining beginning in 1903. In 1983, LTV's Northwest Ore Division leased what remained of Stephens from U.S. Steel and shortly after began digging in the Donora pit. The ore was washed at the nearby McKinley Extension washing plant and either trucked a short distance to the main LTV plant at Hoyt Lakes for loading into cars of LTV's own railroad and transport to its dock at Taconite Harbor, or loaded into DM&IR cars at the Stephens Yard loading pocket. The DM&IR accessed the Stephens Yard via a short spur off the Western Mesaba Branch mainline just east of Aurora. In 1991, this mine's last full year of digging, it shipped 5,141 tons of coarse lump ore through the Duluth docks and 2,790 tons by all-rail routes. There remained sufficient crude ore in stockpile to keep the McKinley Extension concentrator in operation into 1992. This production was shipped exclusively via LTV's railroad and dock at Taconite Harbor.

Small amounts of natural ore continued to be shipped over the Missabe until 1994; Premier Aggregate's Connie Mine north of Virginia shipped from 100,000 to 500,000 tons a year over the Silver Lake Branch.

In 1994 mining began at the dormant Auburn Mine, which had been passed over in the height of natural ore mining due to the location of DM&IR's Minnewas Yard (an extension of the larger Rainy Junction Yard) and Oliver Iron Mining Company's Rouchleau Ore Processing plant on top of these grounds. The Rouchleau facility and Minnewas Yard had long since been removed and the Rainy Junction Yard had been reduced to just a couple of tracks. The mine was reactivated by the Auburn Minerals Company, a partnership between Edward Kraemer & Sons, Inc., a Wisconsin-based mining and heavy construction firm; A.B. Skubic, Inc., a Virginia-based construction company; and Premier Aggregates, also of Virginia, Minnesota.

The primary recipient of Auburn ore was U.S. Steel's Gary Works in northwest Indiana. In fact, U.S. Steel owned the mineral rights to the Auburn property and hired the Auburn Minerals group to mine it for them. Initially, trainloads of Auburn ore were sent to Two Harbors for loading into Great Lakes boats.

However, the moisture content of the unscreened ore made dumping at the dock difficult. So in late fall 1994, three trains were sent on an all-rail routing to Gary, Indiana, via the DM&IR, Wisconsin Central, and Elgin, Joliet & Eastern. The following year, most Auburn Mine ore took this same all-rail route to reach the mill, but in 1996 a drying/screening plant was constructed at the Auburn Mine to solve the moisture problems, and dock shipments through Two Harbors resumed as originally intended. As the mine expanded north and west, it became necessary to relocate a portion of the DM&IR's Virginia Branch in 1996.

No less than three Baldwin diesel-powered mine trains, and a like number of electric shovels, are illustrated in this postcard view of Oliver Iron Mining's operations in the Rouchleau group of pits near Virginia. Ore mined here fed the nearby Rouchleau crusher and beneficiation plant located near DM&IR's Rainy Junction Yard. Mining at Rouchleau ended in 1978; by then, Oliver Iron Mining was known as U.S. Steel's Minnesota Ore Operations Division. ***Pete Bonesteel collection***

The Auburn Mine shipped over 300,000 tons in 2000, all of which was sent by lake boat through Two Harbors to U.S. Steel's Gary Works. The Auburn Mine, which to date remains the last natural ore operation on the Mesabi Range, exhausted its supply early in 2002 and shipped from stockpile for the

remainder of the shipping season. The final ore train from Auburn operated on September 21, 2002, with a Keenan Switch job pulling the last loads from the mine area. The Security Mine, near the old Thunderbird South Mine operated by EVTAC Mining, was later explored for development, but it was discovered that the ore had too high a sulfur content for steel production. Although additional natural ore reserves are scattered throughout the Mesabi Range, as of this writing none are being actively mined.

When natural ore mined at the Auburn pit proved difficult to handle through the ore docks at Two Harbors, managers opted to move the last three trains of the season in all-rail fashion to the Gary Works in Indiana. The trains were taken to Superior and handed off to the Wisconsin Central for forwarding to the EJ&E for final delivery. Since the loaded cars were already in the yard at Two Harbors, the trains were moved from there down the former Lake Division Line operated by the North Shore Scenic Railroad to Duluth. One of the three all-rail Gary-bound trains is seen along the lakefront in Duluth on October 20, 1994. ***Mike Cleary***

The arrival of the 20 SD40-3s would spell the end for the remaining high-nosed SD9/SD18 fleet, which were all stored by late August 1998. SD18 No. 189 heads up a fluxstone train at Mountain Iron en route to Minntac on the morning of October 9, 1999. *John Leopard*

CHAPTER SIX

MODERN OPERATIONS

Unit Taconite Trains

The ability afforded by taconite pellets to run unit trains greatly simplified DM&IR operations. No longer was there a need for the numerous locals, mine runs, transfers, and switching assignments found throughout the Iron Range. In the 1990s, Duluth handled pellets made at the Fairlane and Minorca plants, while Two Harbors concentrated on Minntac's production. When DM&IR began handling fluxstone destined for Minorca through its own facilities at Duluth in 2001,

Minorca pellets were shifted to Two Harbors. Missabe Division–assigned train crews based at Proctor Yard can operate to any of the three taconite plants (all of which have a loop track), load their train, and return to Proctor within the federally mandated 12-hour on-duty time constraint. The Hill Ore job then forwards the pellet loads down Proctor Hill to the Duluth docks where a waiting dock switch crew spots the cars for dumping.

During cold months, pellets can occasionally freeze in the cars at Proctor Yard while they wait to be moved to the docks. To circumvent this problem, the Missabe uses what it calls the "quick dump" mode of operation. Instead of the road crews reporting to Proctor, they report directly to Duluth Dock No. 6, take an empty train north, load it, return to the dock, and spot the train for immediate unloading. The pellets are then stockpiled on the ground adjacent to the dock. Since these trains operate through Proctor Yard without stopping, there is no need for a Hill Ore job, which is thus abolished during the winter months.

With an autumn backdrop, SD38AC No. 207 leads a train of fluxstone past the passing siding at Coons on October 8, 1991. The DM&IR quickly adapted to its changing traffic base as the natural ore deposits played out and taconite pellets took over as the leader in tonnage handled. The movement of fluxstone became an offspring of the taconite pellet-making process when steel makers found it more advantageous to add the limestone/dolomite mixture at the pellet plant rather than the blast furnace. ***John Leopard***

A trainload of fresh, steaming pellets baked at Minorca negotiates a curve on DW&P track just north of Virginia on a cold February 1, 1981, behind SD38-2 No. 209. Missabe wanted more SD38s and by the time they got five more of them in 1975, the SD38AC had been replaced by the SD38-2 in EMD's catalog. *Robert C. Anderson*

Iron Range Division crews running out of Two Harbors operate in a similar manner by going from Two Harbors to Minntac or Minorca and returning. These crews are referred to as Interdivisional or I/D runs, a name that stems from these crews operating through the traditional crew change between divisions at Gilbert. Prior to 1992, trains were exchanged between Iron Range and Missabe Division crews at Biwabik, with the Keenan-based Missabe Division crew taking the train from Gilbert to Minntac or Minorca for loading and returning to Gilbert, where a waiting Iron Range Division crew took the loaded train to Two Harbors.

Various power combinations and numbers of cars per train have been tried on the T-Bird crude-ore runs over the years. Perhaps most prevalent were 86-car trains, with larger 96-cars trains also operated for a short period. Single locomotives powered the T-Birds during the summer months, and in the winter two-unit combinations were utilized to ensure a quicker recharge of the train's air brakes and to aid overall operations in the extreme cold. In the mid-1990s, the two-unit practice was extended to the summer months as well. In this August 10, 1992, scene, a single SD38AC No. 207 has a loaded T-Bird in tow near Keenan and is being passed by an all-rail Geneva train of C&NW coal hoppers en route to the Minntac plant for loading. *Otto P. Dobnick*

T-Birds

At the Eveleth Taconite (today United Taconite) mine and pellet plant, trains popularly known as T-Birds haul raw taconite rock 10 miles from the company's Thunderbird Mine to the Fairlane pellet plant. Initially, mining began along the Virginia Branch near the old Rainy Junction Yard, a location that became known as the North Pit after 1976 when Eveleth Taconite's expansion brought on a need for more ore. To feed increased ore requirements, the South Pit was opened along the mainline at Spruce on the former Duluth, Missabe & Northern Biwabik Branch. Trains at both the North and South pits were loaded using stub-end tracks, while a loop track was used to unload trains at Fairlane.

Mining operations ceased at the South Pit in October 1992 because the easy-to-mine ore was exhausted and the remaining taconite was beneath 70 to 100 feet of rock overburden. To replace the taconite ore previously supplied by the South Pit, Eveleth Mines leased the old Auburn Mine property from U.S. Steel. Located adjacent to the Thunderbird North Pit, Auburn contained easy-to-reach taconite ore in addition to its previously discussed natural ore reserve.

All-Rail Ore

Not all Mesabi Range taconite is destined for mills convenient to transport via the Great Lakes—DM&IR also delivers trainloads of pellets to connecting railroads at Superior for further delivery. The term "all-rail" is used to describe these movements that bypass traditional routing through the ore docks. While all-rail movements were common throughout the Missabe Road's existence, especially when the Great Lakes were closed due to winter ice conditions, year-round all-rail movements have increased since the early 1980s. All-rail unit trains can be found operating to steel mills as far away as Birmingham, Alabama, and Geneva, Utah, as well as Ohio, Pennsylvania, and the Chicago area. The modern era of all-rail movements brought about a kaleidoscope of colors to the railroads, as run-through motive power predominated on these trains. Locomotives from connecting carriers

Beginning in the mid-1980s, run-through power on the all-rail trains made things quite colorful along the Missabe Road. Wisconsin Central and BNSF motive power mingle at the north end of Steelton Yard on January 5, 2001. Steelton Yard is used as the interchange and staging point for most of the all-rail trains. *David C. Schauer*

In 1994 the Southern Pacific teamed up with the Wisconsin Central and wrested the Geneva Steel all-rail contract from the C&NW/Union Pacific. A key reason for the SP/WC combination was that they could backhaul coal mined in Utah and Colorado to utilities in the Midwest, a service the UP could not offer because many of the coal mines UP served in southern Wyoming had closed by the early 1990s, leaving them to haul the empty cars all the way back to Minntac and thus reducing revenue. Early morning July 29, 1995, finds an empty Geneva all-rail train near Keenan behind a WC power consist of a former Santa Fe F45 and two SD45s. *John Leopard*

such as the Chicago & North Western, Union Pacific, Burlington Northern/BNSF, Southern Pacific, CSX, and Wisconsin Central could be seen far from their typical regions. Most of these trains consisted of older 100-ton, bottom-dump steel coal hopper cars. In a few instances DM&IR and even BN/BNSF ore cars were utilized.

Other Products for Taconite Producers

Missabe does much more than haul taconite pellets to Lake Superior. Minnesota's iron mining companies expanded their product lines to meet the demands of different methods of steel production. In an echo of the past, some mining companies produce many different grades of pellets to suit their different customers, each type made to exacting specifications. Other specialized products, such as blast-furnace trim and filter cake, are also shipped in regular Missabe ore cars. Blast-furnace trim, also known as siliceous rock, is crushed, raw taconite high in silica content that is added to the steel-making process to improve furnace operation by increasing slag output. Filter cake, also called concentrate, is basically unpelletized iron concentrate used as a heavy media in a coal beneficiation process, making the coal burn cleaner.

In addition, Premier Aggregates, a partner in the aforementioned Auburn natural ore mine, operated three ballast rock plants: one near the North Pit of the adjacent Thunderbird Mine, one along the main lead into Minntac, and one east of Minntac's East Pit along the DW&P. Crushed waste rock from the adjacent taconite mine was loaded into railroad ballast hopper cars and used by the Missabe, DW&P, Canadian National, and Grand Trunk Western in track-maintenance programs. Front-end loaders were employed to load both the natural ore and ballast materials into the waiting railcars.

Hauling fluxstone presented new operational challenges, resulting in differing scenarios to get it to the plants. With the fluxstone dock at Duluth, and with Minntac pellets normally handled through Two Harbors, Missabe arranged for a backhaul of Minntac pellets to Duluth to increase car utilization by eliminating the return of empty trains. In 1988, Minntac began receiving two 50- to 55-car fluxstone trains each day between the months of April and October using regular ore cars. These trains were manned by road crews out of Proctor that took the trains to Minntac, unloaded them, reloaded them with pellets, and returned to Proctor.

Because fluxstone freezes into large clumps that do not pass through bottom-dump ore cars, Minntac receives their stone via a fleet of side-dump cars treated with an agent called glycol that keeps the stone from freezing to the bottom of the cars. Today, Minntac receives a pair of 35-car trains each day, with these trains returning empty to Proctor Yard.

When Minntac ceased rail-haul of its crude ore, a large number of Difco-built side-dump cars were deemed surplus. DM&IR purchased and rebuilt 123 of these cars in 1998 and 1999, providing a large enough fleet of side-dump cars to deliver Minntac fluxstone year-round instead of utilizing regular ore cars or leased side-dump cars during the warmer months. Daily operations were also changed to include one 58-car side-dump limestone train instead of two 35-car trains. This eliminated

Continued on page 126

Caboose C-217 is about to clear the DW&P diamond crossing at Ramshaw on the Biwabik Branch. The first cabooseless train ran on the Missabe on December 10, 1984, and by the close of 1986 cabooseless operations were fully implemented. The DW&P completed its line through here in 1912, and a tower once controlled this crossing. ***Tom Murray***

215
215

Left: Missabe SD38-2 No. 215 and two stablemates accelerate out of Proctor Yard on November 29, 2002, trailing 58 side-dump carloads of limestone destined for Minntac. The crew will unload the cars, which will then return empty to Proctor. The Proctor diesel shop and yard office are seen in the far distance. *Kevin Madsen*

Below: Missabe's train movements are not limited to solid strings of ore cars. Its journey from Two Harbors is nearly complete as the September 27, 1986, run of the Miscellaneous Road Freight (MRF) arrives in Proctor. Missabe SD9 No. 158 leads an assortment of engines and freight cars as an inbound train of pellets is weighed on the far track. *Robert C. Anderson*

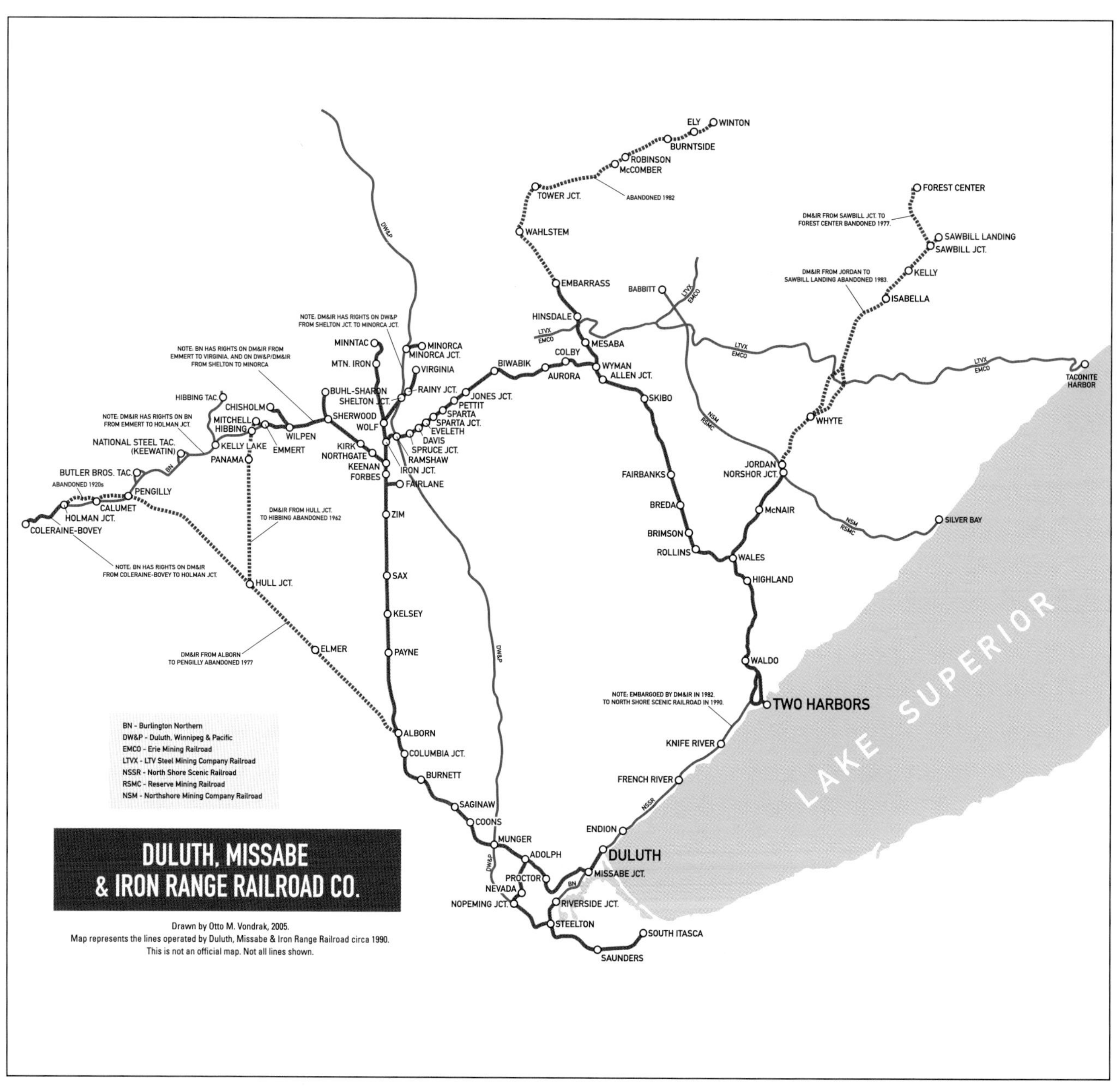

the pellet back-haul to Duluth, and virtually all of Minntac's pellet production is shipped via the Two Harbors docks.

The Minorca plant is not equipped to unload side-dump cars, so their limestone supply is shipped in mini-quad ore cars. This means all of Minorca's stone requirements for the year are sent to them during the warmer months. At first, blocks of 40 to 48 cars of limestone were added to the head end of empty trains bound for Minorca. Once at Minorca, these cars were swapped out with the previous day's now-empty limestone cars, and the whole train, normally 132 cars, is loaded with pellets and returned to Proctor.

When the Bulk Materials Receiving Facility (BMRF) at Duluth expanded to receive fluxstone for Minorca, eliminating the need to transload at Hallett Dock, there was no longer enough room to stockpile Minorca pellets at BMRF. As a result, Minorca's pellet production

The SD18 was EMD's evolutionary successor to the SD9, with an additional 50 horsepower and many significant internal improvements over the model it replaced. Externally, the SD18s were nearly identical to Missabe's last order of SD9s. Heading for the Minorca pellet plant on October 13, 1990, SD18s 193 and 187 are aided by SD9 No. 144, as they roll a train of 48 fluxstone loads on the head end and 76 empty ore cars trailing. This train is pictured just west of Saginaw. *John Leopard*

was sent to Two Harbors, thus requiring new ways to transport Minorca's fluxstone—nearly 300,000 tons a year when pellet production is high—from Duluth. One method of accomplishing this task is to have an empty pellet train destined for the Fairlane Plant take a cut of fluxstone from Proctor to Fairlane or Keenan, where the cars are set out and forwarded to Minorca by a Keenan Switch crew.

MRF and Other Freight Traffic

After the 1982 closure of the Lake Division line between Duluth and Two Harbors, all freight traffic between these two points had to be routed via the Iron Range Division, through Biwabik and Allen Junction. An assignment known as the Miscellaneous Road Freight (the MRF) was created. This train typically operates from Proctor to Two Harbors on Mondays and Thursdays, returning on Tuesdays and Fridays, sometimes Saturdays.

All types of traffic are handled by the MRF. The Missabe benefits by hauling not just pellets but also the raw materials used in pellet production, including bentonite, a sticky clay used as a binder to hold the

On an August morning in 1991, a pair of SD-Ms leads an eastward MRF at the west end of Biwabik. The trackage leading into the distance seen over top of the train is the former D&IR line to McKinley and Virginia. The empty bulkhead flats in the train are destined for the Louisiana-Pacific wood-products plant outside of Two Harbors. *John Leopard*

taconite pellets together, and the steel rods and balls used to crush the taconite ore. Side trips up the Wales and Hinsdale branches to service Reserve/Cyprus/Northshore Mining and LTV Steel Mining, respectively, are common on the MRF. In addition, several explosives plants scattered across the Iron Range (to meet the blasting needs of taconite mining operations) receive carloads of raw materials, namely ammonium nitrate, utilized in the manufacture of explosives.

Despite the preponderance of timber in northeastern Minnesota, the DM&IR has hauled a limited amount of wood products to market in its modern history. In 1964, the J. C. Cambell Company opened a sawmill at Waldo, just north of Two Harbors. The mill was sold to Midwest Timber in 1986, but rail traffic from the mill declined until its sale to the Hedstrom Lumber Company in 1996 revived rail shipments using center-beam flatcars. Citing low lumber prices and a desire to concentrate operations at its flagship mill in Grand Marais, Minnesota, Hedstrom shut down the Waldo operation in April 2001.

Another wood-products operation near Two Harbors has fared better. In the summer of 1985, the Louisiana-Pacific Corporation opened a mill that produces hardboard exterior house siding. This plant shipped its first carload on June 19, 1985, and continues shipping by rail, mainly using center-beam bulkhead flatcars. The plant is reached via a short spur off the southward track at Milepost 2.

A Missabe transfer run bangs across the diamonds of the double-track Burlington Northern (former GN) line just south of Superior at M&J Crossing in 1985. This train is returning from Soo Line's nearby Stinson Yard after performing interchange duties and is en route back to Proctor via the Interstate Branch. In 1986 these diamonds were replaced by turnouts and the tower razed. The exchange of cars between the DM&IR and Soo Line (Canadian Pacific after 1992) was later shifted to Missabe Junction in Duluth, thus negating the need for this transfer operation. *Otto P. Dobnick*

Coinciding with the area's population growth spurred by the opening of the Erie Mining and Reserve Mining taconite plants, the Minnesota Power & Light Company opened this 110-megawatt-capacity, coal-fired, electric-generating plant near Hoyt Lakes in 1953. It soon became an important DM&IR customer, receiving coal by rail. It is reached by a stub end spur that branches off the Iron Range Division mainline at the Colby station. *Basgen Photography, Dan Mackey collection*

In March 1985, the train-dispatching office and all other north-end transportation department personnel were moved from Iron Junction to an expanded yard office at Keenan. On the spring morning of April 17, 1992, BN's Kelly Lake Local arrives at Keenan Yard to drop off interchange cars as Missabe SD-M No. 315 idles in front of the yard office. *Robert C. Anderson*

The Steelton Switch, an assignment operated out of Proctor Yard that runs the length of the Interstate/Spirit Lake Branch, provides an outlet for freight traffic. This job normally operates on Wednesdays and Sundays with its main function to interchange cars with the Chicago & North Western and Wisconsin Central railroads at South Itacsa. A large share of interchange with the C&NW is bentonite clay loaded at Belle Fourche, South Dakota, and Colony, Wyoming.

Coal is another bulk commodity shipped via the DM&IR. In addition to the coal dock at Duluth, Missabe handled coal shipments to power plants on the Iron Range at Virginia and Colby, near Aurora. The low-sulfur coal was mined and loaded into unit trains in the Power River Basin in Wyoming and Montana. Virginia Water and Light, a pint-sized municipal steam power plant located in its namesake city, received small amounts of western coal until July 24, 1999, when the facility began to receive coal trucked from Superior, Wisconsin, where it is off-loaded from trains at the Midwest Energy Resources Corporation. BNSF unit trains deliver Powder River Basin coal destined for Minnesota Power's Laskin facility to Keenan Yard with Missabe's Keenan Switch crew handling smaller cuts of cars to the power plant.

For many years Burlington Northern's (and later BNSF's) Kelly Lake Local, a.k.a. the *Range Rocket*, has called on Keenan Yard on Wednesdays and Fridays, delivering interchange traffic. This train operates via the previously discussed trackage rights over the Missabe from Emmert. Most of the cars delivered are coal for the Virginia municipal power plant and covered hoppers loaded with bentonite clay destined for the Minorca pellet plant. BN/BNSF has rights all the way to the Minorca plant to deliver bentonite. Freight cars are also exchanged between the Missabe and BN/BNSF at Rices Point Yard in Duluth.

Operations Control and Dispatching

When the Merritts first formed the DM&N in 1892, Iron Junction served as its first operating headquarters. For a time, operating control of the railway was transferred to Proctor, but in 1962 a new central operations center was opened at Iron Junction. At that time a new

Caboose No. C-217 brings up the rear of a northbound train of empty cars as the train traverses the east leg of the Iron Junction wye track and heads toward Biwabik in 1961. This depot structure was built by the DM&N in 1892 and was destroyed by fire in November 1973. *Basgen Photography, authors collection*

console-type CTC machine was installed to control 83 miles of track, including 90 remote-controlled power switches. The dispatcher's office was relocated from Iron Junction to Keenan in 1986 and a new CTC console built by Harmon Electronics was installed at that time. In 1986, CTC controlled movements between Allen Junction and Iron Junction, from Milepost 51 on the Missabe Division mainline to Minntac, and the Interstate/Spirit Lake Branch from Nopeming Junction to South Itasca. An updated computerized dispatching system marketed by Alstom was installed at Keenan in April 2002.

In unsignaled territory, main-track movements were authorized by train orders. Track Warrant Control (TWC) replaced train order operation in July 1986, and a computerized TWC system was put online in February 1991. This program, assembled by DM&IR personnel, was patterned after similar systems on sister U.S. Steel line Union Railroad, as well as on BN and Union Pacific. The DM&IR utilized the Consolidated Code of Operating Rules until late 1992 when it was replaced by the General Code of Operating Rules.

Centralized Traffic Control (CTC) was first installed on the DM&IR in 1943 to help expedite movements in the Keenan–Iron Junction–Wolf Junction corridor. With wartime traffic at its peak, up to 90 train movements passed through this area in each 24-hour period. This traffic control machine at Iron Junction was completed by the opening of the 1960 ore-shipping season, as were extensions of CTC signalling between Wolf and Wilpen, Keenan and Sherwood, Mountain Iron and Wolf, and Aurora and Largo. *Basgen Photography, author collection*

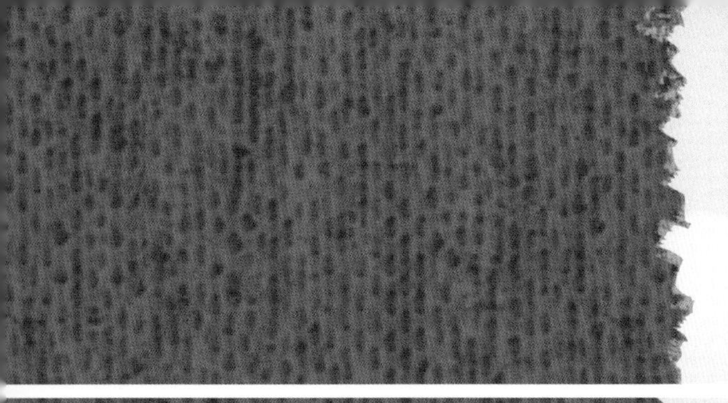

Teamed with SD38-2 No. 210, unit No. 321, an SD-M rebuilt from SD18 No. 187, leads a loaded Minorca "E-rail" train at the south end of Steelton Yard on February 1, 1996. As seen here, outside-braced C&NW ore cars were utilized for this move. These trains were loaded at the Minorca plant and interchanged to the Wisconsin Central at Steelton Yard. WC then forwarded the trains to Escanaba, Michigan (hence the "E" designation), where the pellets were loaded into Great Lakes vessels destined for Inland Steel's (later Ispat-Inland) Indiana Harbor Works at East Chicago, Indiana. *John Leopard*

CHAPTER SEVEN

MISSABE HORSEPOWER

At the time of its formation in 1937 and 1938, DM&IR inherited a varied collection of steam locomotives employed by its predecessor companies. The majority were constructed by Baldwin Locomotive Works, with smaller numbers erected by Alco, Brooks, and Lima. Along with 0-8-0 and 0-10-0 switchers there were 2-8-0 Consolidations and 2-8-2 Mikados for road service, plus 4-6-2 Pacifics for passenger trains. As tonnage grew from the demands of World War I, larger 2-10-2 Santa Fe-type road engines supplemented these engines.

Santa Fe–type No. 500 rests near a water standpipe at Proctor on May 16, 1959. Baldwin delivered six of these 2-10-2s (Nos. 500 through 505) to the DM&N in 1916 to help with the increased tonnage spurred by World War I. Ten more Santa Fes (Nos. 506 through 515), arriving in 1919, were built by Alco's Brooks Works. The 500s were originally acquired to power mainline ore trains, but after the Yellowstones arrived in 1941 and 1943, they were bumped to heavy switching, transfer, and local freight service. No. 500 is preserved at the Museum of Transportation in St. Louis, Missouri. *Robert C. Anderson*

The Santa Fes were an immediate success, pulling trains of 135 cars versus only 65 cars for the Consolidations they replaced.

Ore tonnage more than tripled on the DM&N between 1900 and 1909. Empty ore cars returning from the Duluth docks to the Proctor Yard up Proctor Hill's 2.2 percent grade were a limiting factor. A 2-8-0 Consolidation could handle 55 loaded ore cars down the hill, but could pull only 28 empty cars on the return trip. Management briefly considered electrifying that part of the line, but management concluded that Mallet-design locomotives could complete the task at a lower cost, and Baldwin delivered eight compound 2-8-8-2s in 1910. The articulated Mallets were capable of pulling 55 empty ore cars up Proctor Hill; after mechanical stokers were applied, the number was increased to 85 empties. Baldwin delivered four additional Mallets, two each in 1916 and 1917.

With the storm clouds of World War II brewing and Missabe's fleet of aging Santa Fe and Mallet types reaching 20 years old, managers recognized a need for additional motive power. To accommodate longer and heavier trains as the nation geared up for war, the DM&IR and Baldwin Locomotive Works collaborated on the design of what became the

Missabe Road's most famed locomotive: the Yellowstone. These giant articulateds came with a 2-8-8-4 wheel arrangement first developed for the Northern Pacific Railway in 1928. NP used them on its mainline along the Yellowstone River in eastern Montana, hence the name. Baldwin delivered eight of the behemoths, classed M-3 and numbered 220 through 227, to the Missabe Road in 1941, and followed up with 10 duplicates, class M-4 numbers 228 through 237, in 1943.

The case could be made that the Missabe had the most interesting roster of steam locomotives of any railroad its size. In addition to its own varied roster, it was the repository for steam power of other U.S. Steel railroads as they dieselized: twenty-six 2-8-2 Mikados

This June 11, 1992, photo is representative of the Missabe's diesel roster at the time: high-nosed SD9 No. 166, SD38-2 No. 215, and rebuilt SD-M No. 316. No. 166 had the distinction of being the last active Missabe high-nose diesel in service when it was leased to LTV Steel Mining's railroad. It was stored in late August 1998, still wearing its faded classic scheme. ***John Leopard***

The first eight M-3 Class Yellowstones were assigned to the Iron Range Division, taking over nearly all of the mainline ore haulage out of Two Harbors. Class M-3 No. 225 tugs a train of natural ore westward at McKinley on October 12, 1956. Fortunately, three Yellowstones have been preserved and can be seen to this day: No. 225 was placed on display at the south end of Proctor in 1963, M-3 No. 227 can be seen at the Lake Superior Railroad Museum in Duluth, and No. 229 is on display near the depot at Two Harbors. *Bud Bulgrin*

from the Elgin, Joliet & Eastern and nine 0-10-2 Union-type switchers from the Union Railroad arrived in 1949, and eighteen 2-10-4 Texas-type engines came from the Bessemer & Lake Erie in 1951. All of these locomotives helped the Missabe move its peak tonnage of almost 50 million tons in 1953, long after most other railroads had dumped steam in favor of diesels.

Diesels Arrive

With its modern and well-maintained fleet of steamers, the Missabe Road was able to postpone the purchase of diesel locomotives. Management was free to ease into the diesel craze by testing various models and making sound decisions on what to buy and when. In 1951, the DM&IR sought proposals for conversion to diesel locomotives from the nation's four major diesel builders: Alco, Baldwin, Electro-Motive Division (EMD), and Fairbanks-Morse. Numerous diesel demonstrators from these companies toured the Missabe throughout the early 1950s.

Though Missabe's operating department took note of the strong performance of the

Above: In terms of power, the DM&IR's 18 Yellowstones developed more tractive effort than Union Pacific's more famous "Big Boy" 4-8-8-4 engine—140,000 pounds versus 135,375. Here, No. 226 chuffs past the Proctor back shops on November 28, 1959. All major work on the Yellowstones had to be performed at the Two Harbor back shop as the transfer table at Proctor was not of sufficient length to handle the giant locomotives. *Robert C. Anderson*

Below: Nine ex-Union Railroad 0-10-2 switching locomotives joined the Missabe's roster in 1949. These Baldwin-built engines were first delivered in late 1936 and early 1937 to sister Union, another U.S. Steel-owned company based in Pittsburgh. They were initially assigned to Proctor Hill as replacements for the Class M Hill Mallets, then later used in ore-sorting and dock-switching service at Two Harbors and Proctor. No. 609 simmers at the Proctor roundhouse. *Iron Range Research Center, Chisholm, Minnesota*

A fleet of 74 SD9s constituted the bulwark of the Missabe Road's diesel roster until 19 SD18s arrived on the property in 1960. With nary a steam engine in sight, this May 8, 1960, photo illustrates that diesels have taken over. Brand-new SD18 No. 185 idles in the company of a number of other Missabe diesels. *Robert C. Anderson*

diesel demonstrators they hosted, the railroad had their reasons to stay with steam. The Missabe was still a seasonal carrier; the expense of diesels couldn't be justified on a railroad that didn't run four months of the year. In addition, the Missabe had a large stable of modern steam power, which had been bolstered by the locomotives received from the Union Railroad, EJ&E, and B&LE. The need

Below: Mikado No. 1330 and a host of other steam locomotives are used in ore-thawing operations at Proctor in the late 1950s. Locomotive No. 1330 was 1 of 26 former EJ&E Mikados that the DM&IR acquired in 1948. Ore-thawing operations were a key reason why steam locomotives kept operating on the DM&IR well after most railroads had converted to diesel. *Basgen Photography, David C. Schauer collection*

for steam locomotives in ore-thawing and sluicing operations was also a big factor in keeping steam locomotives.

In a small way, the Missabe entered the diesel era in 1953 with the purchase of its first diesels, 15 EMD SW9s that primarily replaced steam locomotives in commercial freight-switching assignments throughout the system. All of the 1,200-horsepower SW9s

To increase visibility at road crossings, the DM&IR began to paint vertical yellow stripes on both ends of its SD9 and SD18 diesels in 1967. On a glorious May 8, 1991, SD9 No. 164 models the nose stripe as it teams up with No. 139 to strain up Proctor Hill with freight cars from Burlington Northern's Rices Point Yard in downtown Duluth. *John Leopard*

were equipped for multiple-unit operation and were delivered in maroon and gold (deep yellow) colors adopted from the University of Minnesota. However, the SW9s proved too light for the Missabe's heavy-duty assignments, even in multiple, and were all off the roster by 1964.

By the mid-1950s the Missabe no longer could ignore the fuel and maintenance savings offered by the diesel locomotive. Dieselization of the road trains began in earnest in 1956 with the arrival of 10 SD9s. Another 20 SD9s arrived the following year. The last two of this order, Nos. 129 and 130, came equipped with steam generators for passenger service. Twenty-eight more SD9s arrived in 1958, in time to help during the heavy-tonnage years of the late 1950s. They weren't enough to displace Missabe's steam, however, and in an effort to lower operating costs, seven FTs, eight F7s, and five GP7s were leased from neighboring Great Northern for a four-month period in 1958. Sister U.S. Steel railroad Bessemer & Lake Erie also helped out; arriving in 1954 for an extended tour of duty were eight B&LE F7s (four A-B sets). In 1958, these units were joined by four more

B&LE F7A-B sets, bringing the total to 16 B&LE F7s hauling tonnage for DM&IR.

Steam was hanging on by a thread when Missabe's final order of 16 SD9s arrived in 1959, bringing the railroad's total number of that model to 74. Supplementing the SD9 fleet were six 2,400-horsepower RSD-15s built by Alco in 1959. These units were purchased specifically to handle the demanding ore-sorting and dock-switching assignments at Two Harbors. The 1960 arrival of 19 EMD-built SD18s (1,800 horsepower), successors to the SD9s, drove the final nail in the coffin for Missabe steam locomotives. Yellowstone No. 222 led Missabe's last steam powered ore train on July 5, 1960. With ore tonnage

In July 1954, after a successful demonstration tour of two Alco-built 2,250-horsepower RSD7s, the DM&IR purchased six 2,400-horsepower RSD15s (DL600B) from Alco in 1959. These units were specifically bought to handle the difficult ore-sorting and dock-switching assignments at Two Harbors. But the Alcos quickly became orphans on a roster dominated by EMD products, and after only five years of service on the Missabe Road they were transferred to the B&LE in 1964. Pictured here are units 54 and 55 positioning ore cars atop Dock No. 2 at Two Harbors. ***Basgen Photography, author collection***

figures dwindling and plenty of diesel power of its own, the Missabe returned the B&LE F7s in 1961.

By the early 1960s, the Missabe Road was hauling an average of 20 million tons each year, far less than the 49 million tons handled just a decade earlier in 1953. With natural ore shipments rapidly falling, the Missabe was

Sweeping around the curve under the Bear Trap Road overpass west of Grand Lake on September 7, 1986, is a train of pellets led by SD38AC No. 206. The "AC" designation reflected the use of an AR10 AC model alternator. Painted in the railroad's new arrowhead scheme, these were the first low-nose locomotives ordered by the Missabe Road. The second main track pictured here did not have much time left—it was removed in 1988. *Robert C. Anderson*

able to transfer numerous diesels to sister U.S. Steel railroads B&LE and EJ&E during the 1960s, a reverse trend from when these roads were sending diesel locomotives to help out the DM&IR. The exodus began with the six Alco RSD-15s and five SD9s going to the B&LE in 1964, followed by four more SD9s in 1965. The EJ&E received four Missabe SD9s in 1968. These transactions were only the beginning of what would become common exchanges among the U.S. Steel–owned railroads. Due to the seasonal nature of natural ore movement, the DM&IR added revenue by leasing surplus locomotives to other railroad companies during the winter months. As year-round taconite movements grew, this practice eventually ceased.

To spell the well-used SD9s and SD18s, the Missabe took delivery of 8 SD38ACs from EMD in 1971. Their arrival allowed 11 SD9s to depart, 6 that year to the B&LE and 4 to the EJ&E, and 1 more the following year to the EJ&E. The SD38ACs were delivered in the new "arrowhead" scheme, first applied that year to SD18 No. 180, and were assigned to the Iron Range Division, where traffic from Minntac was on the increase. The higher tractive effort of the SD38ACs over the older SD9s and SD18s proved useful on the Two Harbors Line, which climbs more than 1,000 feet above Lake Superior in its first 14 miles. In addition, the Two Harbors Line has three grades of 0.62

A former Elgin, Joliet & Eastern SD38DC, now Missabe No. 221, heads up a train of Minntac-produced pellets at Gilbert on July 26, 1995. Starting in 1992, the DM&IR would receive eight additional SD38-type diesels, four each from the EJ&E (DM&IR Nos. 214 and 221 through 223) and the B&LE (DM&IR Nos. 200, 216, 217, and 225). *John Leopard*

percent against loaded trains, versus one grade of 0.30 percent on the Duluth Line. Running times were also improved as a result of the SD38ACs higher horsepower, resulting in fewer instances of crews running up against their hours-of-service limit.

The improving economy in 1973, and the departed SD9s, sent the Missabe shopping for big power in a hurry. All of the nation's railroads were in need of power, and EMD's order books were full. The Missabe placed an order for 5 SD38-2s, but EMD could not promise delivery until 1975. As a temporary solution to its needs, Missabe purchased 10 Alco-built C-630s from the Union Pacific. These were the only C-630s on UP, and they were not well regarded due to what that railroad considered excessive maintenance requirements. The DM&IR ran the big Alcos out of Proctor in yard and transfer services that kept them close to the diesel shop. According to plan, once the 1975 order of SD38-2s arrived, the C-630s were sent to sister U.S. Steel railroad Quebec Cartier Railway, which maintained a large Alco (built at Montreal Locomotive Works) fleet—three left in 1974, and the remaining seven departed in 1976.

By 1979 the bulk of the Missabe's units were entering their third decade of service. Realizing that the SD9s and SD18s wouldn't last forever, the Missabe borrowed several SD40s from the Duluth, Winnipeg & Pacific for tests on ore runs. They performed fine, but

To compare differing operating and maintenance costs between their locomotive fleets, in March 1980 the DM&IR swapped SD38-2 No. 210 for B&LE No. 892. The orange-painted unit was dubbed "The Pumpkin" by Missabe personnel, who even went so far as to paint a pumpkin on its air-filter box. The tests proved that no significant cost differences existed between the two roads, and the swap became permanent, although No. 210 did return home in late 1992. No. 892 was renumbered 215 and painted in Missabe maroon and gold in May 1989. On a January 3, 1982, morning No. 892 leads a pellet train at Adolph. *Robert C. Anderson*

the cost of new power and the added expense of turbocharger maintenance were deemed too high. Studies were instead conducted on the feasibility of rebuilding the SD9s and SD18s.

SD9 No. 174 was chosen as the pilot model for the rebuilding program, conducted at the Proctor Shops. Its 16-567C prime mover was overhauled and updated with 645 power assemblies. The main generator, traction motors, and trucks were also overhauled. The electrical system was completely replaced with a new Dash-2 electrical cabinet fabricated at Proctor, the short hood was chopped, and a second fuel tank was added to double fuel capacity to 2,400 gallons. The unit got a new number, 301, and a new model designation, SD-M (with the "M" standing for "Missabe," not "Modified"). Its success led to SD9 No. 160's rebuild as SD-M 302. Due to the 1980 recession and resulting depressed state of the steel industry, the rebuild program was suspended.

By 1988 business had picked up to the point that the DM&IR decided to rebuild five more SD-M units at Proctor. The new program did not include the expensive Dash-2 electrical cabinet fitted to the 301 and 302,

Missabe's 10 former Union Pacific Alco Century 630s (UP Nos. 2900 through 2909) were used primarily in yard and hill ore train service. They were based out of Proctor, where mechanical personnel could keep a close eye on the troublesome 3,000-horsepower units. While on the DM&IR, the C630s retained their UP yellow paint with maroon "DM&IR" reporting marks; their numbers were changed by simply blanking out the first digit of the UP number. In this photo, No. 909 switches loaded cars of natural ore at Proctor in July 1974. *Patrick C. Dorin*

In anticipation of a future purchase of reconditioned locomotives, during the second half of September 1995, DM&IR tested two SD40-2CLCs from Helm Financial, numbers HLCX 6051 and 6052. These units were upgraded for Helm by VMV Enterprises and led to the acquisition of 20 reconditioned 400-series locomotives. Pictured here at Mountain Iron, the two HLCX demonstrators are in the company of Missabe SD-M No. 308 and SD38-2 No. 209. Steam rises off the loads of freshly baked pellets from Minntac on this cool September 23, 1995, morning. *John Leopard*

Consecutively numbered SD-Ms 316 and 317 have a loaded T-Bird run well in hand as they twist through the reverse curves on the two-main track territory between Iron Junction and Wolf on September 26, 2004. With United Taconite reopening the Fairlane pellet plant and its associated Thunderbird Mine in December 2003, the DM&IR reactivated five of its stored SD-M units to handle the increased business. These units had been put into storage after EVTAC Mining Company shut down operations in May 2003. ***Kevin Madsen***

though some of the more troublesome relays were replaced with solid-state components. A total of 22 SD-M units were remanufactured at Proctor, all rated at 1,750 horsepower.

With its fleet of SD9 and SD18 models aging, management had a decision to make: continue with the SD-M rebuild program or consider the purchase of newer, higher-horsepower locomotives to meet future needs. The factors influencing the decision to go with larger diesels was twofold: first was a planned three-for-two unit reduction in the number of locomotives per train; second was the need to increase the speeds of loaded trains on the Iron Range Division so a single crew could consistently make the roundtrip from Two Harbors to Minntac within the federally mandated 12-hour on-duty time limit.

In September 1995, the Missabe Road hosted two 3,000-horsepower SD40-3 demonstrators supplied by Helm Financial. They were equipped with a computerized wheel-slip and engine-operating system developed by Woodward Governor and marketed under the name CLC (Computerized

A long way from the tunnels of the Southern Pacific, rebuilt SD40-3 No. 404 leads a train of Minntac pellets on October 2, 2004. The location, known as Lauren, is located just south of Highland. The major aspect of the 400-series locomotive remanufacturing process involved replacing the units' original 20-cylinder, 3,600-horsepower diesel engines with 16-cylinder, 3,000-horsepower powerplants. *Kevin Madsen*

Eighteen of the Missabe's 400-series diesels were first constructed as SD45T-2s for the Southern Pacific Railroad and its Cotton Belt subsidiary. Nicknamed "Tunnel Motors," the locomotives were designed to keep engines from overheating in the numerous tunnels and snow sheds found throughout Southern Pacific's western U.S. routes. Hot exhaust gases tend to collect near the roof of a tunnel or snow shed and are drawn into the locomotive's radiator cooling area—especially the trailing engine in a multiple-unit consist—resulting in the unit overheating and shutting down. The Tunnel Motor design placed the radiator intakes along the rear walkways, instead of on the roof, thus drawing cleaner and cooler air into the radiator from a lower level and at a faster rate once outside the tunnels and snow sheds. Tunnel Motor No. 417 is framed by the trestlework leading to Dock No. 5 on April 28, 1999, as it pulls a string of empty ore cars from Dock No. 6. The low trestle in the background carries the track down to Missabe Junction and downtown Duluth. *David C. Schauer*

Two of the 20 SD40-3 rebuilds (Nos. 416 and 418) utilized SD45-2 shells of Seaboard Coast Line heritage versus the Tunnel Motor body style found on all other DM&IR SD40-3s. As such, units 416 and 418 do not have the open radiator-intake grille along the rear walkway. This June 2004 view of a northward empty ore train at Keenan amply illustrates the differing radiator fan arrangements at the rear of each locomotive. *Kevin Madsen*

Locomotive Control). CLC was a microprocessor-driven system that featured wheel-slip control for better adhesion, included fuel-saving dynamic brake control, provided safe operation of traction motors in short-time capacity, and continuously monitored all critical engine-room functions.

Favorable test results of the demonstrators from Helm led to a long-term lease of 20 SD40-3 units to be delivered in four separate five-unit orders. Performing the actual rebuild work for Helm was VMV Enterprises of Paducah, Kentucky, which utilized 18 former Southern Pacific and Cotton Belt (SSW) EMD-built SD45T-2 Tunnel Motor carcasses. Rounding out the total of 20 units were two former SD45-2 types of Seaboard Coast Line heritage, all equipped with the CLC package.

The first order of five SD40-3s arrived in January 1996, with the final five delivered in late December 1997. Except for the six Alco RSD15s retired in 1964 and the temporary ex-UP C630s, these were the first DM&IR locomotives with turbochargers.

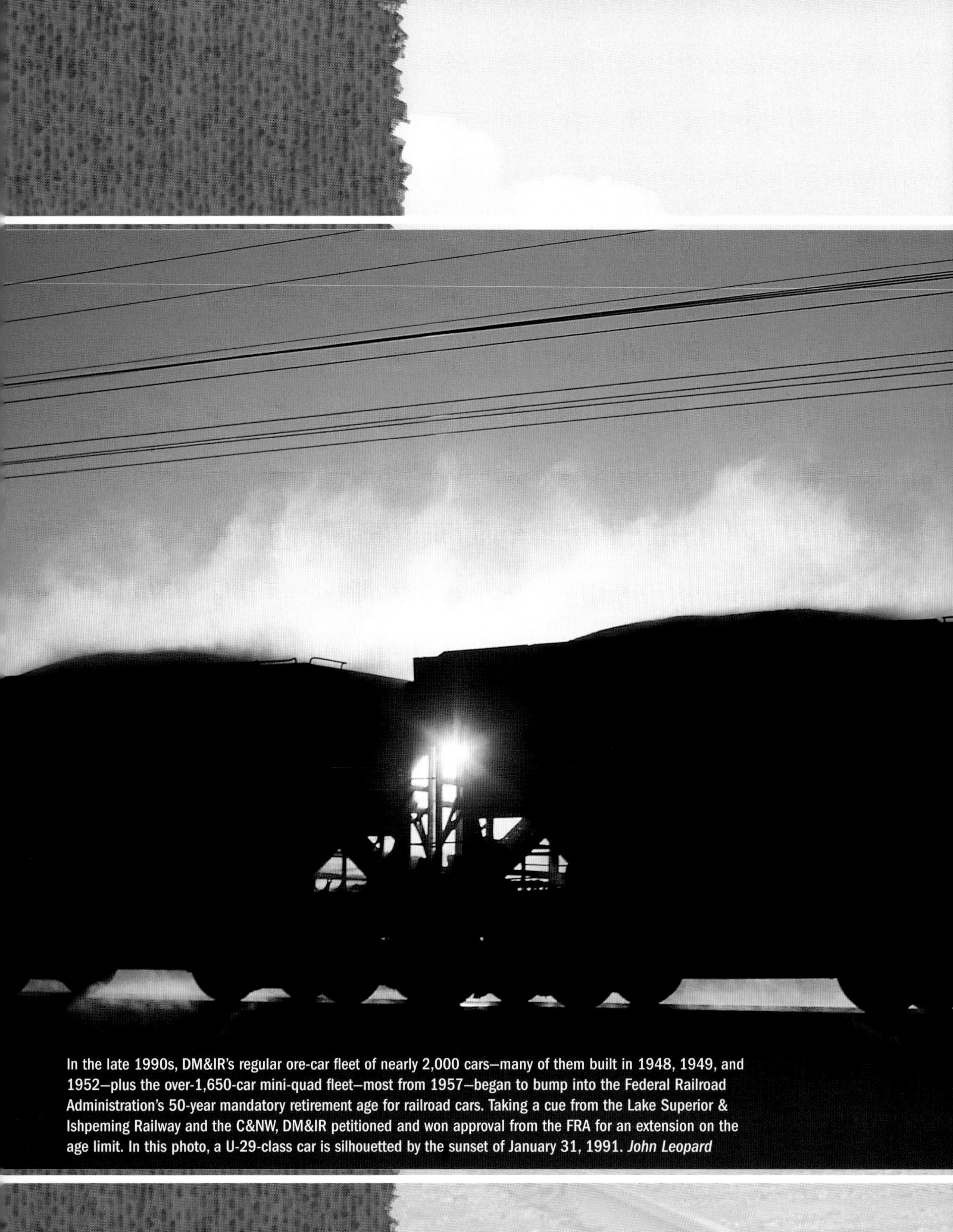

In the late 1990s, DM&IR's regular ore-car fleet of nearly 2,000 cars—many of them built in 1948, 1949, and 1952—plus the over-1,650-car mini-quad fleet—most from 1957—began to bump into the Federal Railroad Administration's 50-year mandatory retirement age for railroad cars. Taking a cue from the Lake Superior & Ishpeming Railway and the C&NW, DM&IR petitioned and won approval from the FRA for an extension on the age limit. In this photo, a U-29-class car is silhouetted by the sunset of January 31, 1991. *John Leopard*

EPILOGUE

As the new millennium dawned, steel makers and pellet producers alike fell upon hard times that rivaled those of the mid-1980s. The heady times of the 1990s were over and the country was in recession. Of 23 integrated mills in the United States and Canada, five owners were in bankruptcy and three others had ceased operations altogether. The so-called minimills now accounted for about half of all domestic steel output.

The steel bridge over the Whiteface River at Kelsey supports the weight of Tunnel Motor No. 410 as it brings a train of ore southward on July 1, 2004. The first order of five Missabe SD40-3s arrived on the property in January 1996. *Kevin Madsen*

A turn of events took place at USX when management decided to refocus the corporation's efforts on steel production. In October 2001, USX Corporation shareholders voted to adopt a plan of reorganization that called for a split-up of its steel-making and energy groups. Its steel-making and other steel-related businesses were incoporated into a freestanding, publicly traded company known as United States Steel Corporation, the name it carried when it was established a century earlier. In a similar twist, the remaining energy holdings of USX became Marathon Oil Corporation.

LTV Steel Mining's operations at Hoyt Lakes had closed in January 2001, after its parent company filed for bankruptcy on December 29, 2000. Two years later, EVTAC closed on May 14, 2003, due to a lack of pellet orders. EVTAC's closure deprived DM&IR of its second-largest revenue producer (behind Minntac) and its largest customer in terms of tonnage. This was a near-fatal blow for the Missabe—in addition to moving EVTAC pellets to the docks, the railroad had also hauled EVTAC's crude ore. Responding to the loss, DM&IR cut 86 people from its 470-person workforce.

The closure of EVTAC left the Missabe Division mainline practically void of trains until an unlikely savior in the form of an expanding Chinese economy, coupled with an improving domestic outlook, fueled an appetite for raw materials. On November 12, 2003, the first of 15 trainloads of taconite to be shipped overseas to China were loaded at Minntac after U.S. Steel contracted to supply 150,000 tons of pellets to the Taishan Iron & Steel Company. The trains were operated in conjunction with Canadian National, which

forwarded the cars from Virginia to Prince Rupert, British Columbia, where the pellets were loaded into an oceangoing vessel.

Even bigger news—or, as one Iron Range politician called it, "a Christmas miracle"—came when another Chinese steelmaker, the Laiwu Steel Group, partnered with North American taconite producer Cleveland-Cliffs to purchase the bankrupt EVTAC Mining Company. On November 26, 2003, a U.S. bankruptcy court judge approved the sale of the EVTAC pellet plant and mine, paving the way for the plant's reopening. The operation was renamed United Taconite. Officials of Cleveland-Cliffs stated that the EVTAC plant would operate at its rated 4.3-million-ton-per-year capacity. In a logistics move, pellets produced at United Taconite were to be sold to North American steel makers, while pellets produced at the Cleveland-Cliffs-managed Wabush pellet plant in Quebec would be shipped to Laiwu Steel in China, due to Wabush's capability to directly load into oceangoing vessels and a shorter shipping distance. Laiwu Steel agreed to a 4-million-ton-per-year contract with Cleveland-Cliffs that would run through the year 2012.

Great Lakes Transportation

In 2001, a corporate reshuffling effectively ended 100 years of direct affiliation between the Missabe Road and U.S. Steel. On March 23, 2001, USX reacquired a number of its former transportation properties from Blackstone. At the time, Blackstone controlled 51 percent of Transtar via its subsidiary named Holdings, with USX owning 49 percent, having bought out the remaining 5 percent share held by senior management. With the 2001 deal, USX took 100 percent control of

A trio of SD38s led by No. 212 clamor through the switch leading to the north wye at Iron Junction on October 1, 1990. This train was earlier loaded at Minntac and is now heading back to Two Harbors. The combined 6,000 horsepower of these locomotives will be taxed by the undulating profile of the Iron Range Division mainline. ***Mike Cleary***

In an effort to test new technologies associated with air-activated door-dumping systems, three manufacturers were called upon to modify a like number of DM&IR ore cars with their door mechanism offerings. In April 2001, all three test cars were together on the head end of an empty train. Each was painted a different color: white is testing a door system made by Johnstown America, the maroon car is testing a Trinity Industries offering, and the blue car is outfitted with a Miner Company system. *David C. Schauer*

Transtar and its transportation properties. Notably absent from this transaction were the DM&IR, Bessemer & Lake Erie, U.S. Steel Great Lakes fleet, and the Pittsburgh and Conneaut Dock Company, which had spun off from Transtar to form a new entity named Great Lakes Transportation LLC, owned by Blackstone's Holdings subsidiary.

Early in 2003, rumors surfaced that Blackstone was looking to unload the Great Lakes Transportation companies. A May 21 article in the *Duluth News Tribune* quoted GLT CEO John Giles as saying that Blackstone had been approached by a prospective buyer, but he declined to identify the interested party. The

story coincided with a reported May 14, 2003, tour of the DM&IR by Canadian National President and CEO Hunter Harrison. Short-line conglomerate Rail America was also reported to be interested in GLT.

Canadian National Takes Over

A summer of rumors and speculation were quelled on Monday, October 20, 2003, when Canadian National announced its desire to buy the rail and maritime assets of GLT. On December 1, 2003, the U.S. Surface Transportation Board (STB) announced that it would treat the deal as a "minor" transaction. On April 9, 2004, the STB approved CN's acquisition plan of GLT, and on May 10, 2004, the world's most famous iron ore-hauling railroad, the DM&IR, was officially purchased by the Canadian National Railway.

The transaction gave CN ownership of the key 17-mile segment of DM&IR's Interstate Branch. An important link in CN's mainline between western Canada and Chicago, this line

The fall colors are in full swing north of Grand Lake on October 3, 1991, as Nos. 209 and 213 rumble down a long tangent with pellets loaded at the Minorca plant. These locomotives represent the first and last engines of the five-unit order of SD38-2s delivered in 1975. ***John Leopard***

Late on a February 2005 afternoon, two SD40-3s, aided by SD38 No. 205, tow 58 heaping loads of fluxstone up the steep grade at Mountain Iron while en route to Minntac. The unique air-brake system of Missabe's fleet of mini-quad ore cars has kept the locomotive fleet largely intact on former DM&IR territory. *John Leopard*

On Iron Range Division ore runs, the 400-series locomotives usually operated in pairs, pulling 116-car trains of mini-quads. On a pleasant August 15, 2002, No. 404 leads Two Harbors–bound pellets near Highland. Like the Missabe Division, the Iron Range Division mainline was once double track, but the second main between Waldo and Allen Junction was lifted in 1964 with passing sidings made at Highland, Brimson, and Fairbanks. *Kevin Madsen*

Canadian National General Electric DASH 9-44CW No. 2581—the first CN train to operate over the DM&IR after the sale was made complete—leads a seemingly endless train of lumber from western Canada across the south switch at Kelsey on May 10, 2004. A key reason for CN's purchase of the Missabe Road was the desire to utilize the parallel mainlines between Nopeming Junction and Shelton Junction for directional running: northward trains via the former DW&P route, southward trains taking the former DM&IR line. *Kevin Madsen*

bridged the gap between the old Wisconsin Central, which CN had purchased in 2001, and CN's longtime subsidiary, Duluth, Winnipeg & Pacific. CN trains formerly ran over this line via trackage rights operated in conjunction with the DM&IR. Ownership of two parallel 64-mile lines between Nopeming Junction and Shelton Junction, near Virginia (previously owned by DW&P and DM&IR, the former plagued with short sidings), would allow directional running and a decrease in train delays.

GLT also owned the Great Lakes Fleet (GLF), a nonrailroad company operating a fleet of eight vessels hauling bulk commodities on the Great Lakes, namely iron ore and limestone. Because a U.S. law known as the Jones Act does not allow foreign-owned maritime companies to carry goods from one American port to another, CN entered into a relationship with Keystone Shipping Company, a Pennsylvania-based firm, to operate the GLF fleet.

After closing the sale on the morning of May 10, the first southward CN train was operated via the DM&IR line between Shelton Junction and Nopeming Junction that afternoon. As of spring 2005, the integration of the Missabe into the CN was barely noticeable from the outside, except for the CN freight trains operating southward on the Missabe Division mainline and a few changes in signage. Due to the air-brake systems of the mini-quad ore cars, the locomotive fleet has been kept intact. The Proctor Diesel Shop continues to perform limited repairs to the fleet, albeit with a reduced staff. Due to the specialized nature of the ore cars and the sheer size of the fleet, almost 2,500 cars total, the car shops remain a viable entity.

SOURCES

Books

Beck, Bill and C. Patrick Labadie. *Pride of the Inland Seas.* Afton, Minn.: Afton Historical Society Press, 2004.

Davis, E. W. *Pioneering With Taconite.* St. Paul, Minn.: Minnesota Historical Society Press, 1964.

Dorin, Patrick C. *Minnesota-Ontario Iron Ore Railroads.* Lynchburg, Va.: TLC Publishing Inc., 2002.

Havighurst, Walter. *Vein of Iron.* Cleveland, Ohio: The World Publishing Company, 1958.

King, Frank A. *Locomotives of the Duluth, Missabe & Iron Range.* Edmonds, Wash.: Pacific Fast Mail, 1984.

————. *The Missabe Road.* San Marino, Calif.: Golden West Books, 1972.

LaBerge, Gene L. *Geology of the Lake Superior Region.* Phoenix, Ariz.: Geoscience Press, 1994.

Lamppa, Marvin G. *Minnesota's Iron Country.* Duluth, Minn.: Lake Superior Port Cities, Inc., 2004.

Miller, Al. *Tin Stackers.* Detroit, Mich.: Wayne State University Press, 1999.

Schauer, David C. *Duluth, Missabe and Iron Range Railway in Color.* Edison, N. J.: Morning Sun Books Inc., 2002.

Walker, David A. *Iron Frontier.* St. Paul, Minn.: Minnesota Historical Society Press, 1979.

Periodicals

CTC Board-Railroads Illustrated. Ferndale, Wash., various issues.

Ore Extra. Duluth, Minn., various issues.

Skillings Mining Review 2004 Minnesota Mining Directory, Duluth, Minn., 2004.

TRAINS Magazine. Waukesha, Wis., various issues.

University of Minnesota Bulletin Mining Directory Issue, Minneapolis, Minn., 1974.

Other Sources

Missabe Railroad Historical Society, www.missabe.com

OreRail@yahoogroups.com

INDEX